PROCLAIMING

THE PROMISE

PROCLAIMING THE PROMISE

Christian Preaching from the Old Testament

by

FOSTER R. McCURLEY, JR.

FORTRESS PRESS   Philadelphia

Library of Congress Catalog Card Number 74-76921

ISBN 0-8006-1083-0

4248B74   Printed in the United States of America   1-1083

To
Martin J. Heinecken
and
In memoriam to
Theodore G. Tappert

CONTENTS

Appendix

SERMONS FROM OLD TESTAMENT TEXTS

PREFACE

The use of the Bible in the life and practice of the church today is severely restricted by what might be called a "verbal inspiration of the final editor." Consciously or unconsciously, many of those who use the Bible in preaching, teaching, and worship regard its present fixed form as the only legitimate means of relating the Scriptures to modern man. Any further probing of the biblical texts is generally left for scholars who are free to discover all kinds of "interesting, but ultimately irrelevant pieces of information."

No one has more clearly stated the position than the popular writer Jacques Ellul. In his preface to *The Meaning of the City*,[1] Ellul makes a "deliberate decision" to disregard the time and place, the diversity of sources and origins of biblical texts, in order to present "an inclusive reading of the text." He cautions against fragmenting the texts and obliterating the meaning by emphasizing "a given word of this revelation to one moment in history . . . so that, completely framed by cultural data, it can no longer be moved from there to mean something else." Yet it is precisely in fixing on "one moment in history"—the moment of the final compiler's work—that Ellul manufactures an "identical, continuous, and coherent revelation" regarding the city which is burdened with exegetical errors and arbitrary interpretations.

It is not the purpose of the present volume to review Ellul's book on the city, or even to speak about the biblical views of the city. Rather it is, in part, to address and challenge the common the-

---

1. Jacques Ellul, *The Meaning of the City* (Grand Rapids, Michigan: William B. Eerdmans Co., 1970), pp. xvii–xviii.

ological and hermeneutical view that the final editors of the Bible are the only, or at least the most legitimate, proclaimers of God's Word. This book does not present a negative response to that position. Rather, it attempts to demonstrate positively the necessity of using all the tools and results of modern biblical research in order to proclaim the word of God to twentieth-century Christians. Far from burdening and confining the present-day interpreter, the scrutiny of biblical texts frees the preacher and opens up for him a wide variety of possible sermons to address the needs of his audience.

A second purpose of the present volume is to discuss this relationship between exegesis and proclamation within the context of the Old Testament. Preaching on the basis of New Testament texts has its own set of problems, but in dealing with the Old Testament we have an entirely new set of questions. What is the relationship between the Old Testament and the New? What role can and should the Old Testament play in the life of the church today? How can obviously ancient Near Eastern sources for many Old Testament stories and customs be reconciled with the unique Christian proclamation of the gospel? What makes a sermon based on an Old Testament text a Christian sermon?

The question of the relationship of the Old Testament to the Christian faith is treated first, for if I do not set forth this position at the outset, the other issues are meaningless. Then I deal with methods and tools for treating Old Testament texts, moving on into an examination of selected texts and their possible uses in Christian preaching. Finally, as an appendix, I include two sermons of my own, in which I have tried to take seriously the principles and methods described in this book. While not intended as examples of homiletical excellence, the sermons demonstrate the deep concern from which I wrote the book.

While accepting full responsibility for the present volume, I must acknowledge that the position described here is the result of continual conversation and ongoing work with my colleagues in the biblical department—Robert Bornemann, Gerhard Krodel, and John Reumann—and with our homileticians Harold Albert and Robert Hughes. Finally, this book is dedicated to Martin J. Heinecken and the late Theodore G. Tappert, my teachers, colleagues, and friends whose influence on these pages is substantial.

Lutheran Theological Seminary   FOSTER R. MCCURLEY, JR.
Philadelphia, Pa.
Easter 1974

PART ONE

THE CHRISTIAN

AND THE

OLD TESTAMENT

Chapter One:

The Old Testament

and the Church

THE CONTEMPORARY SITUATION

1. THE OLD TESTAMENT AND HOMILETICS

Preaching the Word of God on the basis of Old Testament texts —in some denominations, at least—has been and remains an oddity. Many pastors confess they can count on the fingers of one hand the number of sermons which they have based on Old Testament pericopes. The reasons they give for this phenomenon are manifold and somewhat legitimate.

In many denominations within the church the Old Testament has traditionally suffered "benign neglect," and as a result there is no precedent for its homiletical or liturgical use in the congregations' worship life. Indeed, in my own Lutheran tradition it was not until the present *Service Book and Hymnal*, published in 1958, replaced the old orders for public worship that an Old Testament lesson was prescribed for weekly reading at the Service. Until this date in most American Lutheran churches only an Epistle and a Gospel had been read, and the same is true of some other denominations as well. Because of that past tradition, even with the present liturgies, many congregations conveniently neglect the Old Testament lesson, continue to omit it entirely from weekly reading, or excise it when celebrating Holy Communion—apparently because that reading is the most disposable item in the liturgy

3

when one is trying to save time. Such a decision, of course, represents a particular theological and hermeneutical position with regard to the Old Testament witness.

Modern biblical science, it is said, is at fault in several ways. The major problem, many argue, is that modern study of the Bible has tended to concentrate on what the texts meant rather than on what they mean. To be sure, by becoming more and more sophisticated, by stressing an insistence on understanding the original meaning of the text through word studies, through the use of the tools and methods of form-, redaction-, source-, and tradition-criticism, by regarding the historical setting as crucial to the passage, biblical criticism has demanded much on the part of the exegete. To some extent biblical study has left the matter at that point —a frustrating point for a pastor or teacher who is attempting to proclaim the Word of God to a Christian congregation or teach a class in the last quarter of the twentieth century. In other words, the refinements in biblical scholarship have placed the preacher in a bind, because while all the modern methods enable him—by spending much time—to determine what the text meant, he becomes frustrated in trying to determine what the text means for the audience he must address in his ministry.

A second problem is directly related to the first. It becomes clear in examining many Old Testament texts that, rather than describing an incident in the life of Israel, the passage turns out to be classified form-critically as a legend, a saga, a myth, a fairy tale, or a fable. Now how can a man with integrity presume to preach about what he knows is only a literary device which is often common with some pagan story or custom? If he is *not* honest about the background and origin of the story but argues that the incident actually happened, he cannot live with himself. If he *is* honest and tells the congregation that such and such a passage is *only* a myth, then he cannot live with them.

Third, the nature of the Old Testament itself presents a problem both in expression and in scope. It is written in the Hebrew language and expressed from the mind of ancient Semites who had concepts of God, man, world, space, and time which are not entirely coincidental to our own. How can a preacher really get to the primary (original) meaning of a passage which is expressive of a mentality alien to his own and to that of his audience? Besides, the Old Testament is so broad; it requires a staggering breadth of knowledge of history, literature, and theology which far exceeds the demands of the New Testament. Rather than covering one century as does the New Testament, the Old Testament spans twelve centuries of literature and approximately eighteen of history. Rather than dealing with the several theologies of the New Testament in twenty-seven books written by even fewer authors, the Old Testament consists of a multitude of thirty-nine books by infinitely more authors and thus points of view. This comparison in no way suggests that the study of the New Testament is any easier than that of the Old. On the contrary, New Testament interpretation presents serious problems of its own which are of little concern in the field of Old Testament. The above contrast is intended only to emphasize the breadth of Old Testament study which itself is frightening and demanding for the interpreter.

For these reasons, among others, to be sure, the Old Testament is not usually a popular source for contemporary preachers. It is my intention throughout this book to deal with several of these issues specifically. Obviously we can do nothing about the scope of the Old Testament—nor should we if we could, because therein lies its richness. But I hope to be able to show that the results of critical exegesis and the tools available for the interpreter today open up for the preacher a wide and varied range of possibilities for proclamation which would be impossible without the tools and results of modern biblical science.

2. THE OLD TESTAMENT AND SYSTEMATIC THEOLOGY

As with preachers, so with systematic theologians, the Old Testament does not suffer from overexposure. In part, this neglect is due to their own theological training, and in part, it is due to some of the same problems which confront the preacher: the scope of the Old Testament, the language problem, and the constant debates on practically every issue due to different interpretations by Old Testament scholars themselves. The systematician who tries to take the Old Testament seriously has as his basic problem deciding which Old Testament scholar he should use as his source, and on which issues.

But often, rather than working through such questions and problems, the Old Testament is subtly ignored as having no profound significance for Christian theology. To be sure, many present-day theologians admit that the Old Testament should be maintained in a theological curriculum and should be studied constantly by the church, because it provides an important historical and cultural background to the New Testament. But beyond this historical and cultural background, too few systematic theologians employ the Old Testament understanding of the operation of the Word of God in history. And, I suspect, some of the reasons for this failure are:

a. The church-state problem: In the Old Testament Israel the nation is the people of God. The relationship of God and his people Israel cannot easily be transferred to the Christian situation where, of course, the people of God and the state cannot be identical. Therefore, the Old Testament may be irrelevant at many points for Christian theology.

b. The concept of salvation and sin: The Greek words *sōzō*, "to save," and *sōtēria*, "salvation," when used in a theological sense in the Septuagint, *usually* refer to the release by God of Israel from oppression of foes or from other external confinement. This understanding is not what the New Testament means by "salvation." In exilic writers, however, especially in Second Isaiah, the terms do point to eschatological deliverance (Isa. 43:1–3; 60:16; 63:9), and in this sense salvation is also used in the New Testament, especially in the Synoptic Gospels and in Paul.[1] Likewise, the understanding of sin in the two Testaments differs in the sense that, in the Old Testament, man *can* keep the law and thus maintain a right relationship with God (see Deut. 27:26), but in the New Testament "no man is justified before God by the law" (Gal. 3:11). The depth and the universality of sin attested in the New Testament can only be understood in light of the revelation of God in Christ and particularly in his act of judgment on the cross.

c. The concept of God: In several places in the Old Testament God is portrayed as a deity who hardly seems identical to the

---

1. See *sōzō*, *sōtēria* in *Theological Dictionary of the New Testament*, vol. VII, ed. Gerhard Friedrich and trans. Geoffrey W. Bromiley (Grand Rapids, Mich.: William B. Eerdmans, 1971), pp. 965 ff.

Father of Jesus Christ in the New. What does a Christian theologian do with the acts of Yahweh in slaughtering the first-born of Egypt (Exodus 12), in commanding the Israelites to allow no Canaanite to live in fighting a Holy War (Deut. 20: 16–17), or in opening up the earth to swallow those who rebelled in the wilderness (Num. 16:31–35)? How can such witnesses to God be reconciled with the One who sent his only Son to die for the sake of the sinner?

It is because of issues like these—issues which are almost too hot to handle in one sense, and issues which are "irrelevant for a Christian who has a more perfect revelation of God" anyway—that all too many modern theologians choose subtly to ignore the Old Testament rather than integrate its witnesses into their systems.

The problem is by no means limited to modern theology. In fact, the problem is almost as old as Christianity itself and has often been more direct than the subtle ignoring of the Old Testament described above. There remains the task of looking back into history to see that at times within Christendom the Old Testament was indeed rejected as having any significance for the church.[2]

THE OLD TESTAMENT IN THE HISTORY OF THE CHURCH

Among the major figures of the past who have virtually rejected the Old Testament from the canon of the church—and thereby perhaps influenced the more popular neglect of it—four names stand out in particular: Marcion, Schleiermacher, Harnack, and Delitzsch.

1. MARCION

In the second century A.D. the church faced its first great heresy in the person of Marcion. Like the Gnostics, he advocated a dualistic notion of the universe with its usual corresponding dualism of good and evil; i.e., the world is evil, because it is material; the heavens which are spiritual are good. Now if the world is evil, then one cannot say that the good God of the New Testament made it. Thus, there must also be a dualism in the gods of the Old

---

2. For a fuller treatment of the lack of use of the whole Bible in the life of the church today, see James D. Smart, *The Strange Silence of the Bible in the Church: A Study in Hermeneutics* (Philadelphia: Westminster Press, 1970).

and New Testaments. The God of the Old Testament, the creator of the world, was not very divine in essence. The God of the New Testament, however, is the highest emanation of divine essence. He is the Christ who came to reveal the hidden knowledge of God and to save man from the evil world of the Demiurge. Since such a sharp dualism of gods was evident between the Old Testament and the New, the Testaments themselves present a dualism. Therefore, Marcion could easily drop the Old Testament from the canon, because this inferior God of the Old Testament, the God who manifested himself in law and justice, was wholly opposed to the gracious and loving God of the New. For these teachings Marcion was excommunicated about A.D. 144.

We must, however, be fair to Marcion. Everything we know about him comes from his opponents (the church fathers) who are obviously biased in their writings about him. It does seem, though, that he understood the Old Testament as being theologically naive, that it spoke of God in anthropomorphic rather than in spiritual terms, in warrior categories connected to a narrow nationalism rather than to a universal understanding of man. Marcion also took seriously Paul's distinction between law and gospel, but he identified these with the gods of the Old and New Testaments respectively. Thus Marcion ended up with a dualism of gods rather than with an understanding of the Word of God (the same God) confronting man with the accusing power of the law and at the same time with the gospel as the forgiveness of sins, the justification of the ungodly.

Because of his complete rejection of the Old Testament, Marcion had to omit from his canon much of the New Testament as well. Any New Testament writer who used the Old Testament witnesses to argue a point was equally naive. His excommunication for this stand meant that the early church itself took a stand on the role of the Old Testament within the church, but what that role is precisely has been a major source of controversy for these many centuries.

2. FRIEDRICH SCHLEIERMACHER

In the eighteenth and nineteenth centuries there were heard voices which sounded very much like Marcion — voices which made sharp distinctions in the religions of the Old Testament and the New, some for theological and some for racial reasons. Among the best known and most influential of these scholars was Friedrich Schleiermacher, who was willing to maintain a cultural and historical relationship between the Testaments but wanted to sever them theologically. "The relations of Christianity to Judaism and Heathenism are the same, inasmuch as the transition from either of these to Christianity is a transition to another religion."[3] Schleiermacher was willing to maintain the Old Testament in the Bible because of its historical and cultural interests, but he felt that its importance for the life and faith of the church should be relegated to that of an appendix.

3. ADOLPH VON HARNACK

Early in the twentieth century this church historian, or historian of dogma, wrote the definitive work on Marcion[4] and apparently regarded himself as a reincarnation of the ancient heretic. Harnack accepted Marcion's major contention that the Old Testament ought to be rejected from canonical rank and, he suggested, placed at the head of the Apocrypha. His most telling remark on the matter is quoted by virtually everyone who writes on his views of the Old Testament. "To have cast aside the Old Testament in the second century was an error which the church rightly rejected; to have retained it in the sixteenth century was a fate which the Reformation was not yet able to avoid; but still to keep it after the nineteenth century as a canonical document within Protestantism results from a religious and ecclesiastical paralysis."[5]

4. FRIEDRICH DELITZSCH

Toward the end of the nineteenth century, Friedrich Delitzsch, along with Eberhard Schrader, laid the foundations for the science which came to be called Assyriology. After working closely with

3. Friedrich Schleiermacher, *The Christian Faith*, trans. H. R. Mackintosh and J. S. Stewart (Edinburgh: T. & T. Clark, 1928), see pp. 60–62.
4. Adolf von Harnack, *Marcion: das Evangelium vom fremden Gott*, 2d ed. (Leipzig: Hinrichs, 1924).
5. Harnack, *Marcion*, pp. 221–222. Quotation taken from John Bright, *The Authority of the Old Testament* (Nashville: Abingdon Press, 1967), p. 65.

the new finds from Mesopotamia, Delitzsch reported some of his discoveries and opinions before the German Oriental Society in the year 1902. The title of the paper he read there was *Babel und Bibel*.

In this paper he said that the Bible was the reason that so much money and energy were being expended in the Orient for excavations of ancient sites. Now with the help of recent discoveries, he argued, one could finally gain a world view which was based on reason and not on Old Testament thoughts about the origins of the world and natural phenomena. One now could develop an ideology which was not in contradiction to reason, for finally it was possible to separate that which was common in the mind of ancient Near Eastern man from what we know to be true today. Bible and Babylon are closely knit together, and in recognizing this to be the case, modern man can finally free himself from ancient knowledge derived from the Old Testament and move to new understanding.

Delitzsch went on to say that, since the Egyptian pyramids and the Assyrian palaces have been excavated, it becomes clear that the people of Israel were the youngest of peoples among more mature neighbors. Seen in this light the Old Testament loses its authority. When the twelve tribes of Israel invaded Canaan, they entered a land which was completely the domain of Babylonian culture. Delitzsch tried to show that Babylonian industry, custom, law, and science were already prevalent in the land. Even religious customs, such as the Sabbath, were derived from Babylonian culture. And, of course, literary dependency was emphasized and illustrated by the familiar creation and flood stories; similarities between the Old Testament and Babylonian stories were striking. According to Delitzsch, Babylon was the light-bringing element; the Old Testament could show light only by reflecting the brilliance of these foreign elements.

Following the expected storm of protest against his position, Delitzsch became even more radical in his judgments, and in this frame of mind he published in 1921 *Die grosse Täuschung* (*The Great Deception*). In this book his pro-Babylonian tendency became more and more polemical against the Old Testament and, in fact, became mixed with an anti-Semitic ideology. In this volume he called the Old Testament erroneous, anachronistic, misleading, contradictory, and above all, full of deceptions which make it a very dangerous book to use.

Delitzsch was a Marcionite through and through, but he was even more dangerous. Marcion argued as a theologian, one influenced by Hellenistic philosophy and particularly by Gnosticism, to be sure, but nevertheless as an academician. Delitzsch, on the other hand, argued as a racist. But in denying that Yahweh of the Old Testament is to be identified with the Father of Jesus Christ (this is "the great deception"), Delitzsch joined Marcion in omitting the Old Testament from the Christian canon.

These four men, in varying degrees, were spokesmen for a position regarding the Old Testament which has been voiced from time to time within the history of the church. Their basic philosophies and presuppositions differed, to be sure. Marcion argued out of a basic Gnostic stance which was centered in a dualistic view of the world. Schleiermacher and Harnack were, to a greater or lesser degree, affected by a Hegelian process of evolution which was influential in many fields in the nineteenth century. Delitzsch combined an overenthusiasm for Assyriology with an anti-Semitic bias to make the most blatant and offensive statements concerning the Old Testament. But all four concluded that the Old Testament held little, if any, theological value for the church. While few today would voice their positions in terms as strong or as clear as these men, nevertheless the "benign neglect" which the Old Testament suffers in the church today cannot be separated from the views of these men.

Chapter Two:

The Two

Testaments

THE OLD TESTAMENT IN THE NEW

The study of the use of Old Testament quotations, images, and motifs by New Testament writers has deservedly received much attention in recent decades.[1] Some of the instances in which early Christian authors used the Old Testament are rather casual. For example, the author of 2 Peter was dealing with the problem of Christians falling back into their old pagan ways. He says it would have been better for a man not to have been a Christian than, having been one, to turn away. And then he says, "It has happened to them according to the true proverb, 'The dog turns back to his own vomit . . . .' " That saying appears at Prov. 26:11 where the dog is compared to "a fool that repeats his folly." Such a quotation is pointed, to say the least; it is humorous to us; and it is casual.

Most of the New Testament writers' use of the Old, however, is

---

1. Among the more important volumes in this area are C. H. Dodd's *According to the Scriptures: The Sub-Structure of New Testament Theology* (London: Nisbet, 1952) which was published in summary form as "The Old Testament in the New" (London: Athlone Press, 1952 and reprinted as a "Facet Book: Biblical Series" by Fortress Press, 1963); Barnabas Lindars's *New Testament Apologetic* (Philadelphia: Westminster Press, 1961); E. Earle Ellis's *Paul's Use of the Old Testament* (Grand Rapids: William B. Eerdmans, 1957); Krister Stendahl's *The School of St. Matthew and Its Use of the Old Testament* (first published as Volume XX of *Acta Seminarii Neotestamentic*: Upsaliensis, 1954; reprinted by Fortress Press, 1968).

much more serious, for it concentrates on attempting to explain the identity of Jesus. The author of Matthew was particularly interested in using Old Testament *quotations* in order to prove who Jesus was and how his name—the same as Joshua—indicates what he was to do: "save" his people. At Matt. 3:3 the author defines the task of John the Baptist by citing Isa. 40:3.

> "The voice of one crying in the wilderness:
> Prepare the way of the Lord,
> make his paths straight."

If John is the preparatory voice in the wilderness, then the one who comes in the same chapter is somehow identified with the Old Testament Lord and with an act of salvation, for the anonymous prophet of the exile whom we call Second Isaiah was announcing the coming of salvation with the approach of Yahweh.

At Matt. 2:6, when Herod was told where the Messiah/Christ was to be born, the scribes read Mic. 5:2 which, in fact, says nothing about anyone's birthplace. It does express, however, that a ruler, a king who is a Bethlehemite would come to Judah to deliver it. In applying this verse to Jesus, the author of Matthew says not only that Jesus is a king of the Davidic line—the Messiah —but that deliverance would come through him.

St. Paul, too, displayed a fondness for quoting the Old Testament in order to present his Christology, and perhaps his most prominent attempt in this regard appears at Rom. 10:5–13, where the apostle uses the Old Testament three times. (1) In verses 6–8 he uses Deut. 30:11–14 to demonstrate that Christ is the word on which righteousness is based and which is near the people; in this passage Paul reinterprets the passage from Deuteronomy which speaks of the law. (2) At verse 11 Paul cites Isa. 28:16 (Septuagint version) where the object of faith is either the precious cornerstone or God himself; for Paul the object of faith is clearly reinterpreted as Christ. (3) At verse 13 he quotes Joel 2:32 which announces salvation for all who worship Yahweh; for Paul, the title "Lord" has been transferred to Christ in whom is centered salvation for all (see verse 9).

In addition to quotations, *stories* were told by the early church in order to proclaim Jesus' identity, and these stories could be understood only on the basis of a knowledge of the Old Testament. One of these stories is recorded at Mark 4:35–41 (Matt. 8:23–27; Luke 8:22–25). Jesus and his disciples were crossing the sea in a boat when a great storm arose and threatened to sink their craft. The disciples, in deadly fear, awoke Jesus who rebuked the wind and calmed the sea. The disciples, we are told, were filled with awe, and came away from the experience wondering, "Who then is this, that even the wind and sea obey him?" Now anyone who heard this story and knew his Bible, i.e., the Old Testament, already recognized who Jesus was. For in the Old Testament there is only one who rebukes the wind and calms the sea: God.

> Ps. 89:8–9: "O Lord, God of hosts, who is mighty as thou art,
> O Lord, with thy faithfulness round about thee?
> Thou dost rule the raging of the sea;
> when its waves rise, thou stillest them."
>
> Ps. 18:15: "Then the channels of the sea were seen,
> and the foundations of the world were laid bare,
> at thy rebuke, O Lord,
> at the blast of the breath of thy nostrils."

If God is the one who rebukes the wind and calms the sea, then the question of the disciples "Who then is this . . ." has already been answered.

Finally, Old Testament *imagery* is used by New Testament writers to announce who Jesus is. Among these is the Good Shepherd passage at John 10:1–18 which can be understood only in light of Ezekiel 34. There is also the Servant of the Lord image used in many places in the New Testament which can best be explained by the Old Testament background of Second Isaiah.[2]

Thus, passages, stories, and images from the Old Testament are used by various New Testament writers (and by the early church) in order to demonstrate, among other things, who Jesus was. While we today shy away from what is often allegorical interpretation of the Old Testament by the early church, nevertheless the use of the Old Testament in the New—particularly in dealing with the identity of Jesus—demonstrates a continuity between the Testaments. Out of the Old is drawn proof for something, or better

---

2. See Walther Zimmerli and Joachim Jeremias, *The Servant of God*, "Studies in Biblical Theology," no. 20 (London: SCM Press, 1957).

someone, in the New. Now it becomes necessary to move beyond the use of the Old Testament in the New in order to deal theologically with the relationship between them in terms, first, of discontinuity, and, then, to return to other aspects of continuity.

THE OLD TESTAMENT AND THE NEW[3]

1. DISCONTINUITY BETWEEN THE TESTAMENTS

One can say that a discontinuity exists between the Testaments in the sense that the New Testament represents a fulfillment of what is only prophesied or predicted or promised in the Old. Just as there is a discontinuity between engagement and marriage, so there is discontinuity between the anticipation of the Old Testament and the realization of the New. The Old Testament anticipates the kingdom of God; in the New it is realized. The Old Testament longs for a Messiah; in the New he has come. The list could go on to demonstrate that the dividing line between Malachi and Matthew is most simply and realistically drawn by the distinction between anticipation and realization, and herein is discontinuity. The time of waiting has ended; the new period has begun.

The discontinuity between the Testaments can also be seen in terms of correction. In the New Testament Jesus Christ corrects concepts and witnesses of the Old. (1) The revelation of God in Christ renders unacceptable the view of the witnesses to a God who slaughters the first born of Egypt, who commands the Israelites to kill off all Canaanites, who opens up the earth to swallow sinners, or who sends serpents to bite them for their murmuring. (2) Also unacceptable, due to the corrective of God's revelation in Christ, is any exclusive nationalism which runs through some of the Old Testament. Even in those passages which portray the participation of all peoples in the kingdom to come, Israel stands apart—at God's right hand—and receives along with God the service of the Gentiles (see Isa. 60:1–6; 61:5–7). (3) The vision

---

3. The relationship between the Testaments and the significance of the Old Testament for the church has provoked lively discussion during the past few decades. Two volumes of essays published in English during the 1960s have presented the views of biblical, as well as systematic, theologians: *Essays on Old Testament Hermeneutics*, ed. Claus Westermann; Eng. ed. James Luther Mays (Richmond, Va.: John Knox Press, 1963); and *The Old Testament and Christian Faith*, ed. Bernhard W. Anderson (New York: Harper & Row, 1963).

of the Messiah itself is corrected in Christ. What the Old Testament looked for in a Messiah was one who would rule over the kingdom when God had established it. This notion became more and more nationalistic and militaristic, and by the time Jesus entered the stage the expected Messiah was such a political figure that Jesus never used the title of himself lest he and his purpose be misunderstood. But the New Testament portrayal of Jesus as the Messiah emphasizes a saving, redeeming role which the Messiah of the Old Testament did not play. Never is Jesus portrayed as an earthly ruler as he was envisioned in the Old Testament. (4) The understanding of priesthood is corrected in the New Testament. In the early period of the Old Testament priestly functions were carried out by the heads of families. In the period of the judges there were Hebrew priests, but these did not seem to be an established institution. In the monarchy under David priesthood became quite rigid, and more and more through the centuries it became a definitely higher class of individuals—almost to the point of deification. In the New Testament however, this separation of priest and laymen is obliterated, and all men who are believers are summoned to be priests. (5) In the Old Testament the land is the material proof of God's blessing and the sign of the fulfillment of God's promise. The land of Canaan became so important that all kinds of theological difficulties developed when the people were exiled from that material sign of the covenant relationship. In the New Testament, however, no such emphasis on geography or any other material object is allowed, for what is important is the relationship between God and man made new in the scandal of the cross. This list could go on to make more contrasts between the Old Testament and the New, but enough has been shown, I think, to demonstrate that the discontinuity between the Testaments can be described in terms of concepts which are corrected by the New Testament witness to God's revelation in Christ.

The discontinuity can also be described as the difference between historical and eschatological. In the Old Testament the people of God is the empirical nation Israel—in the New Testament the people is a community of the last days; the church is a prototype of the community of the eschaton; it is non-empirical,

non-nationalistic! The same is true of the covenant and the kingdom of God. In the Old Testament these are empirical, i.e., within
history; in the New Testament they are eschatological.[4] In general,
all the Old Testament prophecies were predictions of the eschaton,
the end time. Insofar as the early church made use of these prophecies, the church displays an eschatological consciousness. Indeed,
the church is already the called and chosen congregation (*qehal
yhwh*) of the end of days—called and chosen through the cross
and resurrection of Jesus, itself an eschatological event since it
ushers in the kingdom of the end time. In other words, the future
is already here in the present, even though the present is also hanging on for dear life. The church, the people of God, the new covenant, the kingdom of heaven—all these are elements of the eschaton to come, and yet they are already inaugurated among us. In
these respects Bultmann is correct. However, he falls short in this
matter on two points: (1) he fails to take seriously the fact that
this eschatological community with all its consciousness of the end
time and with its insistence on not being *of the world* is nevertheless at the same time *in the world*. Therefore, the sharp contrast
between the history and the eschatology of the Testaments respectively can be misleading if this tension is not maintained; (2)
Bultmann regards the historical-empirical as virtually negative
from a theological viewpoint. To this problem of a positive theological view of history we shall return.

Thus, there are three ways in which the discontinuity between
the Testaments can be explained: (1) the emphasis on the time of
realization over against the prior time of anticipation; (2) the
corrective of the New Testament revelation of God in Christ; (3)
the contrast between the historical-empirical and the eschatological.
The use of the Old Testament in the New forces one to deal with
these discontinuous elements.

But all this stress on discontinuity presents only half of the picture, and to stop here would result in Marcionism. Now we must
return to discuss the continuity between the Old Testament and the
New.

4. See Rudolf Bultmann, "Prophecy and Fulfillment," trans. James C. G. Greig,
in *Essays on Old Testament Hermeneutics*, pp. 50–75.

2. CONTINUITY BETWEEN THE TESTAMENTS

In almost contradictory fashion, a continuity exists between the Testaments in the sense that the New Testament represents a fulfillment of what is prophesied or predicted or *promised* in the Old Testament. In spite of all the exegetical problems, in spite of New Testament allegorization of Old Testament texts, nevertheless the New Testament writers indeed saw that *the* event of the New Testament is related to the witnesses of the Old Testament. The basic relationship is that the same God is operating in both, that Yahweh of the Old Testament *is* the Father of Jesus Christ. But beyond that identification, the continuity can be expressed in terms of what that same God is *doing*: What he promises in the Old Testament he fulfills in the New. Now this is precisely what was said to point to a discontinuity. But it goes both ways. The same thing promised in the Old Testament God fulfills in the New. There is a continuity, as well as a discontinuity, between engagement and marriage. Anticipation and realization cannot be separated; they can only be distinguished!

The historical-eschatological problem must enter into the matter of continuity also, for while the Christ event is an eschatological event, nevertheless it must be historical, i.e., it must have happened. There is no point in arguing for the soteriological significance of the cross if this carpenter of Nazareth had not died on it in space and time. Thus in the New Testament, as well as in the Old, God acts *in* history to accomplish his purposes, to unfold his will—and this is crucial for continuity. In the Bible we have one God working through men and in spite of them to accomplish his purpose, one God operating in and between the categories of promise and fulfillment, one God to whom all the witnesses point. History is thus the arena of revelation, but this history with which the Bible is concerned is the history of the Word of God breaking into the affairs of men and creating history anew!

Now there is a particularly significant result of those two notions. The continuity which exists between the Old Testament and the New does not exist between other religions and the New Testament. For in the Old Testament there is a view of history and of God which is unknown elsewhere outside the New Testament. History as the unfolding of the will of God from promise to fulfillment is unique in the Bible.[5] God who is not the sought but the seeker is unique in the Bible; i.e., in other religions men strive after God, reach out to him, seek him; in the Bible God strives after men, reaches out to them, seeks them, and ultimately dies on their behalf. Thus, in the Old Testament there is a continuity with the New Testament which does not exist elsewhere, and this continuity can be defined in terms of an understanding of God and of history.

Continuity between the Testaments can also be described in Bultmannian terms as the existential situation in which man finds himself without God; i.e., in the Bible all human endeavor—history—only leads to frustration, for it leads to a miscarriage and drives men to the need for a savior.[6] This existential understanding in the Old Testament is a preparation for the gospel of the New.

Biblical motifs common to the Old and New Testaments are also a sign of continuity. Though Hebrew is used in one Testament and Greek in the other, the words for word, righteousness, grace, love, law, mercy, wrath, etc. provide a whole study in themselves which shows that the proper cultural, as well as theological, background for many crucial themes in the New Testament can only be understood and interpreted in light of the Old Testament. This is not to say that nothing is developed in these motifs in the New Testament beyond what they signify in the Old, and it is not to say that every New Testament motif can be understood from an Old Testament perspective. For example, the understanding of sin is radically understood in the New Testament in light of the person of Jesus the Christ, and the New Testament revelation adds a depth of understanding to sin which is not possible on the basis of the Old Testament itself. Or again, the important notion of life after death in terms of resurrection of the body is only hinted at in the Old Testament, and only *clearly* so in the late book of Daniel (chapter 12). The New Testament understanding of resurrection

---

5. See Hartmut Gese, "The Idea of History in the Ancient Near East and the Old Testament," trans. James F. Ross in *The Bultmann School of Biblical Interpretation: New Directions?* vol. I of *Journal for Theology and the Church*, ed. Robert W. Funk (New York: Harper & Row, 1965), pp. 49–64.

6. Bultmann, "Prophecy and Fulfillment," pp. 73–74.

from the dead is thus not a consistent development from the Old Testament.

But in spite of these and other motifs in which the New Testament witnesses surpass the Old or even introduce new ideas, much that is important for the New Testament understanding of God and man and the relationship between the two is derived from the Old Testament and that points to a continuity between the two Testaments.

Thus, continuity between the Old Testament and the New has been described in terms of promise-fulfillment, the revelation of God in the arena of history, the existential situation of man, and the use of biblical motifs. Now we come to the problem in which continuity and discontinuity come into contact with the categories of law and gospel.

3. LAW AND GOSPEL IN RELATION TO CONTINUITY AND DISCONTINUITY

The topic of law and gospel in relation to the Testaments is put into sharp focus by Rudolf Bultmann in his essays "Prophecy and Fulfillment" and "The Significance of the Old Testament for the Christian Faith."[7] Because of the sharp and crucial nature of his arguments, Bultmann deserves much attention in this entire chapter. In both of his essays he makes clear what he means by regarding the Old Testament as law, even though he uses somewhat different terms and images. The Old Testament is a "miscarriage of history" or a "history of failure" which he demonstrates to mean "the recognition that it is impossible for man to gain direct access to God in *his* history within the world, and directly to identify *his* history within the world with God's activity."[8] This is to say that fulfillment cannot be regarded as the consequence of historical development, that by his deeds man does not attain righteousness, a right relationship with God. And with that assertion we heartily

---

7. The first of these has been referred to above. The second, "The Significance of the Old Testament for the Christian Faith," appears as the first essay in *The Old Testament and Christian Faith*, ed. Bernhard W. Anderson, pp. 8–35. The following twelve essays in this volume are intended to serve as responses—direct or indirect—to Bultmann's position.

8. Bultmann, "Prophecy and Fulfillment," p. 73.

agree! Moreover, insofar as this failure to attain direct access to God convicts man, accuses him, makes him aware of his creatureliness before the Creator, there is no real problem in accepting this failure as law, as the "tutor unto Christ" (Gal. 3:24). When Bultmann goes beyond this to say that this miscarriage (equals law) is present outside the Old Testament, although the Old Testament provides the traditional and clearest understanding of law as the pre-understanding of the gospel, we also agree. In regarding this accusing law as similar to natural law, Bultmann stands in the company of Paul and Luther.

However, some qualifications are necessary, for Old Testament law is not simply identical to natural law:

In the Old Testament the law is given by the covenant God who is the New Testament's Father of Jesus Christ. Unlike natural law, Old Testament law is given by the same God who comes in the New Testament to die in his son on Calvary. Set within the covenant (Sinai) context in the Old Testament, the law is given to that people which has *already* been redeemed and elected, and so while the *content* of law, e.g., the Ten Commandments, might be quite similar to natural law, the *context* is different—even unique. The law is given to Israel *not* in order to gain access to God but because he has already provided that access through his elective and redemptive act at the Reed Sea. It is this same God who in the New Testament—likewise in a *unique* way—makes a *new* covenant and a *new* covenant people.

Related to the same God-in-covenant notion is the belief that the Old Testament law is not simply a set of principles derived from natural law and observation, from universal morality and desire. Rather Old Testament law is the demanding *personal will* of a God who has established a people for himself. Thus, natural law for a Canaanite, e.g., is different, because in that religion —as in many others—God *is* nature essentially or the basic power in nature. Law then is simply what is consistent with the natural order of things. But for the Old Testament, where God is Lord *over* nature, a personal will provides the norm and the yardstick, thus law.

There seems to be something unique about Israel's miscarriage of history over against the miscarriage of natural law, for according to Paul the failure of Israel under the law means riches for the world, for the Gentiles (Rom. 11:12), and because of her trespass or miscarriage, Israel's rejection means reconciliation for the world. This miscarriage of which Paul speaks is the failure of Israel to worship Jesus Christ as Lord, and by their rejection, the mission of the gospel spread to the Gentiles who thereby experienced reconciliation. This failure has nothing to do with an Old Testament incident, but according to Paul it is the *climactic* "miscarriage" by which the gospel is spread to the nations. In this sense there is something special, even unique, about the failure of Israel.

What I have been saying then is that Israel's law (which is miscarriage of history) is not identical to natural law. However, it can be said to have basically the same *function* as natural law; i.e., to reveal to man the hopelessness of trying to reach God by human means and thus to drive men to the need of a Savior whom we confess to be Jesus Christ.

Thus, insofar as the Old Testament is law, it has a crucial theological function. However, in achieving this function it is not unique. And so it is only because the Old Testament is clear in its expression of law and is traditional within the history of the church that Bultmann concedes it is good to maintain the canon. It is preparation for the gospel in that it reveals sin and drives men to Christ.

But is this all that the Old Testament is? Is the Old Testament significant for Christians only because it is law? For Bultmann, there is gospel in the Old Testament, but it is meaningless for us: Old Testament gospel is not gospel to us.[9] Thus from a Christian's point of view, Bultmann says, the Old Testament is *only* law, and this law is the miscarriage of Israel's history, and that miscarriage is promise. Now with this fourfold equation there are a number of problems.

First, the identification of Israel's miscarriage of history with the Old Testament is an erroneous oversimplification. The Old Testament is not a history book about a nation whose course can be diagrammed on a downward slanting line. The Old Testament is not

about Israel as the subject. Rather it is a book, or rather a collection
of books, about God as the subject and about Israel as the willing
or unwilling object. The Old Testament is a history of the Word of
God which moves from promise to fulfillment, a Word which is
not divorced from the concreteness of Israel's historical existence
but which is not identical to that nation's political, ecclesiastical, or
cultural involvements. Just as we previously argued that the Old
Testament God is not identical to nature but Lord over nature, so
also it must be said that the Old Testament God is not identical to
history (even Israel's history) but Lord *over* history. God reveals
himself *not as* history but *in* history, and in confronting man in
time and space he may create a new thing or turn things around.
But he *is* not history in general or any nation's history in particular. Now Israel's history, like anyone's history, miscarried, failed
—and so it is law. But to say that the Old Testament as a whole is
law because it is miscarriage is to say that God failed, too—that his
working *in* Israel's history did not achieve the fulfillment of the
promise, that God's plan did not work, that the confrontation of
his Word has no effect! This is the difficulty in failing to distinguish the history of the Word of God in the Old Testament from
the history of Israel.

Second, the equation of the miscarriage of history with promise
is a most peculiar piece of logic. According to any dictionary,
"promise" is always positive, denoting one's pledge to another, a
ground for hope or assurance. Promise is not despair, not God-forsakenness, not hopelessness. Moreover, in Bultmann's equation of
miscarriage and promise, the genitives seem to be confused—perhaps again because of the failure to distinguish Israel's history
from the history of the Word of God: what is necessary here is to
ask *whose* miscarriage and *whose* promise. The answer can only be
formulated: Israel's miscarriage; God's promise. And in so doing,
the two cannot be equated or even identified. In fact, the only way
the two concepts can enter the same sentence is to say that "*in spite
of* Israel's miscarriage of history, God's promise is maintained in
the Old Testament and reaches fulfillment in the New Testament."
Such a sentence stresses a contrast between the two—certainly not
an equation. But for Bultmann who stresses the preparation (*Vor-*

verständnis) of the Old Testament as law, the word *promise* can have no other meaning than this peculiar illogical definition as "miscarriage."

This *Vorverständnis* of the Old Testament law is theologically significant for Bultmann because it reveals man's existential plight without God. But it is precisely this existentialism which prohibits Bultmann from seeing anything more than pedagogical value to the Old Testament which, again, is Israel's miscarriage of history. It is only because man asks who he is that history has significance, because in history he can find out how he got to be who he is. This is a legitimate question for an existentialist to ask, and frankly it is a question with which any one of us should deal. But the imposition of the hermeneutical existentialism on the Bible presents a number of problems. In the first place the questions of existentialism are not the questions of the Bible, for the subject, or at least the starting point of existentialism, is man, whereas the starting point for the Bible is God. Second, the man of existentialism is a particular man—me—and the emphasis is on the individual. In the Old Testament the emphasis is on Israel and ultimately on mankind, and in the New Testament on the unique person of Christ, then on the eschatological mankind, and on the new Israel, the church. Third, history for existentialism is merely pedagogical in that it teaches a man how he came to be who he is. But history in the Bible is the confrontation of the Word of God in the arena of space and time in which God effects his plan for mankind—whether I know it or not. That is to say, biblical history is not simply a matter of cognition; it is the effect and activity of God's Word. Something *happened* on the cross which is effective whether *I* know it or not. Now it is the effectiveness of event that is lacking in Bultmann's existential hermeneutic. While he rightly distinguishes *Historie* from *Geschichte*,[10] he separates the two to such an extent that the Bible seems to be a book of *ideas about God* rather than a book of the witnesses to the effects of God's Word in history. Now it is true that Bultmann regards God's eschatological act of salvation in Christ as the key to his whole theology, and that

---

10. In German *Historie* is that which can be reconstructed from the past on the basis of historical science, whereas *Geschichte* is the whole reality of the past, visible and invisible, which is interpreted from a particular viewpoint.

seems to put him on the right track. But when Bultmann goes beyond distinguishing to separate this event from history,[11] one wonders whether the gospel is simply an idea which strikes one's eschatological or existential consciousness. But even if Bultmann would take seriously the cross as a historical event, it surely would be the only historical event worth anything more than pedagogy, and that in itself presents problems. Granted, the cross of Christ *is* God's act of redemption; it is really all that is *needed, essential* for salvation. But how can *one* act, even though absolutely unique, even though scandalous, even though of eschatological import, be an isolated act—isolated, that is, from the Old Testament witnesses in particular and from the situation in which it happened. If the crucifixion stands alone, i.e., without the Old Testament, then one must conclude that it was purely accidental. that Jesus was a Jew, that the crucifixion took place in the city of Israel's temple where the cross *was* such a scandal (cf. Deut. 21:23). If this unique Christ event was not an accident in space and time, then the Old Testament must be taken more seriously as a *Vorverständnis* than any other literature or culture or nation or natural law. Because *the* event of the Bible is preceded by other events in the Old Testament, even that event cannot be interpreted in a vacuum. In other words, if Jesus came as a Persian, then we would probably have to consider Zoroastrianism more important than Israel's Scriptures as *Vorverständnis*. But since he came as a Jew in Israel, then even though what was accomplished was new and unique, we must seriously consider Israel's testimony to God as more significant than any other background—not only because of clarity and tradition but because of theological continuity.

Now we must question whether the Old Testament is only law and the New Testament is only gospel. For Bultmann, this equation comes to the fore in all clarity, and he puts himself in good company when he says that in Paul and in Luther the Old Testament as a whole appears under the concept of law, but New Testament man stands under the divine grace which accepts him as a

---

11. "The message of the forgiving grace of God in Jesus Christ is not a historical account about a past event, but rather it is *the Word which the Church proclaims*, which now addresses each person immediately as God's Word and in which Jesus Christ is present as the 'Word' " ("The Significance of the Old Testament for the Christian Faith," p. 30).

sinner.[12] It is not surprising that when scholars of other traditions critically review Bultmann's position, they immediately label his law-gospel/Old Testament-New Testament antithesis as Lutheran. Indeed, one can demonstrate that at times Luther said much the same thing. However, in identifying Luther's position in this way, Bultmann and others present only half of the picture. For Luther, law and gospel are not divided vertically between the Testaments but run parallel horizontally through both Testaments.

> There is no book in the Bible that does not contain both. God has placed them side by side in every way—law and promise. For he teaches through the law what there is to do, through the promise whence it should be taken. But the New Testament is primarily called gospel above other books because it was written after the advent of Christ, who fulfilled God's promise and through oral preaching publicly disseminated that promise which was before hidden in the Scripture. Insist, therefore, upon this difference; and read whatever book is before you—be it Old or New Testament— with such a difference so that you may notice: where there are promises, that is a gospel book; where there are commandments, that is a law book. But because there are a heap of promises in the New Testament and a heap of commandments in the Old, we call one the gospel book and the other the law book.[13]

In fact, it has been shown recently that the equation of the law with the Old Testament and of the gospel with the New is one of the features of medieval hermeneutics that Luther overcame, and that the promise in the Old Testament was practically synonymous with the gospel.[14]

Luther, of course, interpreted the Old Testament christologically. The prophecies of the coming Christ, the Messianic passages,

---

12. Bultmann, "The Significance of the Old Testament for the Christian Faith," p. 14.

13. *Sermon on the Third Sunday in Advent on Matt. 11:2 ff., Advent Postil,* 1522, *WA* 10[1.2], 159:7; *LE* 10,100. Quotation is taken from Heinrich Bornkamm, *Luther and the Old Testament,* trans. Eric W. and Ruth C. Gritsch; ed. Victor I. Gruhn (Philadelphia: Fortress Press, 1969), p. 83.

14. J. S. Preus, *From Shadow to Promise: Old Testament Interpretation from Augustine to the Young Luther* (Cambridge, Mass.: The Belknap Press of Harvard University Press, 1969), pp. 2, 5, 191, 223. Also see Paul Althaus, *The Theology of Martin Luther,* trans. Robert C. Schultz (Philadelphia: Fortress Press, 1966), pp. 86 ff.

point to the gospel, and so they are gospel. But the gospel, under-stood in light of the New Testament, pervaded the Old Testament quite apart from these individual prophetic passages. Luther, for example, finds the gospel in the Old Testament where reference is made to a "new law," as in Isa. 2:3: "For out of you shall go forth the law, and the Word of the Lord from Jerusalem." This univer-sal law would be the dissemination of the gospel through the apos-tles; the law here meant proclamation.[15]

Most important, however, in his dynamic understanding of the Word of God as law and gospel is Luther's interpretation of the First Commandment. "I am the Lord your God" is the promise of promises which embraces the gospel of Christ. At the same time, depending on how the hearer is struck by this promise of God, the commandment could result in either judgment or comfort and thus become law or gospel. But here once again, promise is virtually synonymous with gospel.[16] Paul, with whom Bultmann identified himself also, *contrasts* law and promise in Gal. 3:10–29 (especially verses 14, 17–18, 29). In the same chapter, Gal. 3:8, Paul identi-fies as gospel the promise to Abraham that "In you shall all the nations be blessed." Admittedly, this verse provides the only occa-sion in which this quotation is termed "the gospel," but Paul comes close to such an equation again in Romans 4. Nevertheless, it is significant that he calls the promise of universal blessing here *to euaggelion.* Paul also defines the gospel as "promised before-hand through his prophets in the holy scriptures, the gospel con-cerning his son . . . Jesus Christ our Lord" (Rom. 1:1–4). Or again, "the power of God for salvation to everyone who has faith, to the Jew first and also to the Greek. For in it the righteousness of God is revealed through faith for faith; as it is written, 'He who through faith is righteous shall live.' " (Rom. 1:16–17). The first of these definitions of gospel is christological, and the second is soteriological: justification of the ungodly in which the righteous-ness of God is revealed. When the two definitions are brought together, the essence of the gospel is the power of God manifested in the Christ event and resulting in God's justifying the sinner. By

15. Bornkamm, *Luther and the Old Testament*, pp. 154–155.
16. Ibid., pp. 165–166, 175, 178.

this understanding one can see why Paul used *to euaggelion* to speak of the universal promise given to Abraham.[17]

With this understanding of the gospel as the universal justification of the ungodly effected in the Christ event and promised beforehand to Abraham, we can speak of gospel in the Old Testament—not because it predicts Jesus in Messianic passages but because in the Old Testament God promises a universal blessing through Abraham which results not in failure but in fulfillment in his Son. We know this gospel from the New Testament, and without the New Testament we cannot even speak of gospel in the Old. Gospel is understood as *the* event by which God justifies the ungodly in Christ, and only on that basis can we speak of the Old Testament as witnessing to the promise of that event. In this sense the Old Testament contained the gospel. In the same way, when Luther virtually identifies the "I am the Lord your God" of the First Commandment as gospel, he does so because he knows what the gospel is in the New Testament witness. Therefore, the proclamation that God is the covenant people's God is assurance of his presence and activity among them. In this righteousness, i.e., in being faithful to this relationship, the gospel is present. While justification is not an Old Testament term, forgiveness, acceptance, righteousness are, and throughout the Old Testament these words and many images proclaim God as one who accepts, forgives, makes righteous the sinner. Since we know the radical nature of this justification from the New Testament, we can see that the same God was acting throughout the Old Testament to accomplish his purpose in the New.

Thus, law and gospel are present in both Testaments, for the Word of God which confronts man in the Old Testament as in the New may be either that which shows man the error of his own way, i.e., the law, or the faithfulness of God to turn a universal curse into a universal blessing in spite of man's ways, i.e., the gospel.

17. For the interdependence of Christology and soteriology in Paul's use of "gospel," see Gerhard Krodel, "The Gospel According to St. Paul," *Dialog* 6 (1967), p. 102.

Chapter Three:

Promise and Fulfillment

as Hermeneutical Categories

A Christian approaches the Old Testament with a committed set of presuppositions. The church is the *new* Israel, the people of the *new* covenant, redeemed by God's act on the cross through Jesus Christ who is not only the world's Savior but its Lord as well. While these presuppositions cannot determine one's exegesis in the sense that they prostitute the original meaning of an Old Testament passage, the meaning the passage has for the church—if any at all—is determined by one's Christian stance. Christians read the Old Testament as New Testament men. Now if we take this theological approach seriously, then in discussing the categories of promise and fulfillment, we must deal with fulfillment first, for that is where we stand as Christians. Only after defining the fulfillment can we move into the Old Testament to see if and how it is actually promise.

FULFILLMENT IN THE NEW TESTAMENT

New Testament writers employ two roots in order to speak of something being "fulfilled." First, the terms *teleioō* and *teleō* are used to designate that something has been "accomplished" or "brought to fulfillment," usually, however, with no mention of an existing promise or prophecy. *Teleioō* is so used in the following passages (my italics):

John 4:34:   Jesus said to them, "My food is to do the will of him who sent me and to *accomplish* his work."

John 5:36:   ". . . the works which the Father has granted me to *accomplish*, these very works which I am doing, bear me witness that the Father has sent me."

John 17:4:   "I glorified thee on earth, having *accomplished* the work which thou gavest me to do;"

1 John 2:5; 4:12, 17, 18: "perfected" in love

Teleō is employed likewise in the following passages (my italics):

Luke 12:50:   "I have a baptism to be baptized with; and how I am constrained until it is *accomplished!*"

John 19:28:   After this Jesus, knowing that all was now *finished*, said (to fulfill the scripture), "I thirst."

30:     . . . he said, "It is *finished*"; and he bowed his head and gave up his spirit.

Rev. 17:17:   "for God has put it into their hearts to carry out his purpose by being of one mind and giving over their royal power to the beast, until the words of God shall be *fulfilled.*"

See also 2 Cor. 12:9; 2 Tim. 4:7; James 2:8.

There are some cases, though, in which *teleioō* and *teleō* are used specifically to point to the fulfillment of Old Testament prophecy or scriptures in general (my italics):

John 19:28:   After this Jesus, . . . said (to *fulfill* [*teleioō*] the scripture), "I thirst."

Luke 18:31–32:   And taking the twelve, he said to them, "Behold, we are going up to Jerusalem, and everything that is written of the son of man by the prophets will be *accomplished* [*teleō*]. For he will be delivered to the Gentiles and will be mocked and shamefully treated and spit upon; and they will scourge him and kill him, and on the third day he will rise."

Luke: 22:37:   "For I tell you that this scripture must be *ful-filled* [*teleō*] in me: "And he was reckoned with transgressors" [Isa. 53:12] for what is written about me has its fulfillment [*telos*]."

Acts 13:29:   "And when they had *fulfilled* [*teleō*] all that was written of him, they took him down from the tree, and laid him in a tomb."

Rev. 10:7:   ... in the days of the trumpet call to be sounded by the seventh angel, the mystery of God, as he announced to his servants the prophets, should be *fulfilled* [*teleō*].

These cases of *teleioō* and *teleō* show that in Johannine and Lukan material there was a particular emphasis on Christ's *fulfilling* or *accomplishing* God's work. By the use of these terms the authors do not always point to a promise; they simply point to the accomplishment of God's will. In the latter cases cited, however, there is a concern for a promise or prophecy to be fulfilled, and in three cases (except Rev. 10:7 and Luke 22:37) the fulfillment has to do with the crucifixion of Jesus. The prophecy for that event seems to center in the suffering servant of Isaiah 53 (which is quoted at Luke 22:37 apart from the crucifixion). It seems that in these Johannine and Lukan references the fulfillment—with or without a stated prophecy—is the suffering of Jesus which is culminated on the cross.

The second root used in the New Testament for the fulfillment of God's work is *plēroō*. In the material peculiar to Matthew we find, phrased in different ways, "in order that what was said through the prophet might be fulfilled" a number of times: 1:22 (citing Isa. 7:14), 2:15 (citing Hos. 11:1), 13:35 (citing Ps. 78:2), 21:4 (citing a combination of Isa. 62:11 and Zech. 9:9). The formula specifically mentions Jeremiah at 2:17 (citing Jer. 31:15), 27:9 (citing Jer. 32:6–15, 18:2–3) and Isaiah at 4:14 (citing Isa. 9:1–2), 8:17 (citing Isa. 53:4), 12:17 (citing Isa. 42:1–4). Similar phrases such as "that the scriptures might be fulfilled," "the scripture had to be fulfilled," "the scriptures have been fulfilled," etc. occur in such places as Matt. 26:54, 56; Mark 14:49; Luke 4:21; 24:44; John 13:18; 17:12; 19:24, 36. Particularly interesting is Acts 3:18: "... But what God foretold by the mouth of all the prophets, that his Christ should suffer, he thus fulfilled. . . ." This passage is interesting because it is the only place where God is explicitly said to fulfill his word by actualizing it; fulfillment is stated more passively in the other cases.

At any rate, the *plēroō* formulae are used most often by Matthew in the infancy stories (1:22; 2:15, 17), the story of the passion (26:54, 56; 27:9), the story of the entry into Jerusalem (21:4), the explanation of teaching the people by parables (13:35), the demonstration that eschatological expectation is fulfilled in the healing work of Jesus (8:17; 12:17), and the reference to Jesus' move to Capernaum (4:14). In all these cases Matthew is attempting to show that God's promise is fulfilled in the person and work of Jesus. In John the formulae are used to relate the details of the passion, but the primary concern there is with the figure of Judas (13:18; 17:12) and the rejection of Jesus by the Jews (12:38; 15:25). In Luke *plēroō* is used at 4:21 to say that the promise of the messenger of good news is fulfilled with Jesus' preaching, and at 24:44 the risen Lord points out that the necessity of the cross and resurrection is based on the whole Old Testament. "These are my words which I spoke to you, while I was still with you, that everything written about me in the law of Moses and the prophets and the psalms must be fulfilled." He goes on to point out the suffering of the Christ, his resurrection on the third day, and the forgiveness of sins to all nations. Thus, the *plēroō* formulae are used exclusively in the Gospels and in Acts to refer to the Christ event. They show that the New Testament concept of fulfillment is summed up in the *person and work of Jesus.*

Therefore, the fulfillment in the New Testament in terms of *plēroō* and *teleioō/teleō* can be described as *the accomplishment of God's will in the person and work of Jesus Christ.* Thus while Paul does not use these *plēroō* or *teleō* formulae, his understanding of the gospel[1] as a combination of Christology and soteriology corresponds to the formulae usage, and we find this understanding of fulfillment throughout the whole New Testament in the same way. This fulfillment cannot be nailed down allegorically to individual passages but rather to that person and his work to whom the New Testament bears witness.

1. See Chapter Two, pp. 41–42.

PROMISE IN THE OLD TESTAMENT

If the fulfillment is described in terms of Christology and soteriology, then finding the promise of that fulfillment in the Old Testament becomes rather difficult, especially if one is not to allegorize (and thus distort) historical documents. If the fulfillment *could* be described in any one New Testament passage which uses an Old Testament proof-text, then, of course, the promise could also be defined precisely by citing that Old Testament passage. But the *teleioō/teleō* and *plēroō* passages we have just discussed seem to portray a number of fulfillments (usually related to the person and work of Christ), and that variety may mean that we must likewise speak of a number of promises in the Old Testament. Those used from the Old Testament came from Isaiah (7:14—the Immanuel passage; 9:1–2—a Messianic prophecy), from Second Isaiah (42:1–4 and 53:4—both servant passages), from Jeremiah (31:15—a judgment passage), from Hosea (11:1—not a prophecy at all but a quasi-credal statement), and from Ps. 78:2 (a historical survey psalm which is no promise at all). In other words, the same promise is not used by the New Testament writers, and some of the passages from the Old Testament do not promise anything at all.

Perhaps if we ignore for a moment the New Testament quotations and concentrate on promise in the Old Testament itself, the picture will become clearer. Philologically the Hebrew language offers some help, but unfortunately there is not a word in Hebrew which specifically means "promise." The Septuagint uses the common *epaggelia/epaggelein* only rarely and then only in late texts (1 Esd. 1:7; Esther 4:7; Ps. 55(56):8; Amos 9:6; 1 Macc. 10:15; 4 Macc. 12:9). When "promise" appears in translation in English, it is usually a rendering for Hebrew *dbr* = to speak or *'mr* = to say. The use of *dbr* occurs in the sense of promise in over thirty cases, some of which are (my italics):

1 Kings 8:20: "Now the Lord has fulfilled his *promise* [*debārō*] which he made; for I have risen in the place of David my father, and sit on the throne of Israel, as the Lord *promised* [*dibber*], and I have built the house for the name of the Lord, the God of Israel." (For the promise see 2 Sam. 7.)

1 Kings 8:56:   "Blessed be the Lord who has given rest to his people Israel, according to all that he *promised* [*dibber*]; not one word has failed of all his good *promise* [*debārō*], which he uttered by Moses his servant." (For the promise see Deut. 12:10).

Exod. 12:25:   "And when you come to the land which the Lord will give you, as he has *promised* [*dibber*], you shall keep this service." (For the promise see Gen. 15:12 ff.; 12:7; Exod. 3:8, 17).

Hebrew '*mr* is used in the sense of promise a number of times also.

Exod. 3:17:   "and I *promise* [*wā'ōmar*] that I will bring you up out of the affliction of Egypt, to the land of the Canaanites, the Hittites. . . ."

Num. 14:40:   And they [the people] rose early in the morning, and went up to the heights of the hill country, saying, "See, we are here, we will go up to the place which the Lord has *promised* ['*āmar*]; for we have sinned." (For the promise, see the preceding passage.)

2 Kings 8:19:   Yet the Lord would not destroy Judah, for the sake of David his servant, since he *promised* ['*āmar*] to give a lamp to him and his sons for ever. (For the promise see 2 Sam. 7.)

The cases cited here point to a number of promises among which are the promise of land, the promise of deliverance, the promise of an enduring dynasty, the promise that a temple would be built, the promise of rest to God's people. But there are a number of other promises in the Old Testament which are proclaimed apart from the terms *dbr* and '*mr*. There is the promise to Abraham of descendants, often accompanied by land and blessing for all the earth, which is emphasized in J, E, and P: Gen. 12:2; 18:18 (J); 15:1–5 (E); 22:17–18 (E); 17:5–7 (P); repeated to Isaac at Gen. 26:3–4 (J), and to Jacob at Gen. 28:13–14 (J). There is the promise of the Lord's presence and guidance to an individual (e.g., Moses, at Exod. 3:12; 33:14) and to the people (the whole wilderness motif). There is the promise of a Messiah (Isa. 9:1–7; 11:1–10, etc.). Any number of promises of salvation are evident (e.g., Isa. 43:1 ff.) and of judgment (e.g., Joel 2). And the list could go on to show even more that the Old Testament might be subtitled "promises, promises."

It is significant that many of these promises are fulfilled in the Old Testament itself. Abraham had his son and became a great nation (Exod. 1:1–7); the people who were slaves in Egypt were redeemed (Exodus 14); the same redeemed people made it through the frightening wilderness by God's guidance (Exodus 15–18; Numbers 10–36); Moses did know the comfort of God's presence until his death (Deuteronomy 34); the exiles were set free and the temple was rebuilt. In the books of Deuteronomy through Kings exists a close correspondence "between the words of Yahweh and history in the sense that Yahweh's word, once uttered, reaches its goal under all circumstances in history by virtue of the power inherent in it."[2] In at least eleven cases in the Deuteronomistic history, Gerhard von Rad demonstrates that a promise of God had been fulfilled.

Of course, there are also promises in the Old Testament which were not fulfilled in the Old Testament: the blessing for all families of the earth (Gen. 12:3; 18:18; 22:17–18; 26:4; 28:14) does not seem to have been described as fulfilled; nor the promise of a Messiah who would rule over a kingdom of universal peace and harmony (Isa. 11; 9:1–6; Zech. 9:9–10); nor the new creation of Isaiah 65–66; the new covenant of Jer. 31:31–34 does not reach any fulfillment in the Old Testament, nor does the ultimate day of Yahweh.

Now if we are to understand promise in the Old Testament, it is clear that it cannot be derived from the fulfillment in a direct sense; i.e., the New Testament fulfillment of God's redemptive act in Christ is not promised in any one of these Old Testament promises *or* in the sum total of all of them—not even those unfulfilled in the Old Testament. Nevertheless, while no particular Old Testament passage can be said to contain *the* promise fulfilled in Christ, it is dangerous to divorce these many promises from *the* promise. These many promises are nothing other than the effects of God's Word in the history of Israel. To ignore them completely, to separate them from *the* promise entirely, is to cut off and destroy the

---

2. Gerhard von Rad, *Studies in Deuteronomy*, "Studies in Biblical Theology," no. 9, trans. David Stalker (London: SCM Press, 1953), pp. 78–81.

concreteness of the Old Testament faith and make of it simply a timeless myth. The growth of a people, their deliverance from the bondage of Egypt and from the exile of Babylon, the possession of the land of Canaan, the enduring dynasty in Jerusalem—these are precisely the concrete acts which are understood as the result of God's Word in Israel. They can be ignored only at the expense of relevance, of concreteness, of history (*Geschichte*). Without them the Word of God in the Old Testament is only an idea, a figment of the imagination. But with them we are still faced with the problem: How can *the* promise be related to these many promises which are so diverse and seem to have little, if anything, to do with the New Testament?

The only answer which can be given is that *the* promise is *not* of *something* but of *someone*: God. The content of *the* promise is not of some coming thing but of him who comes to be with his people.[3] *The* promise is no different from the promiser! Yahweh gives the promise of himself, that in his Word he comes to be present with his people. But if that is all there is to say, we end up with a strange kind of spiritualism, in fact, a kind of mysticism where the goal of religion is to be with God (whatever that might mean). It is at this point that the concreteness of the Old Testament with its many and varied promises becomes crucial. When God comes in his Word, something happens! His Word effects things, confronts men, changes directions. His Word by which he comes is dynamic, and it is in dynamic confrontations that God effects deliverance, judgment, and various means of relating to his people (cult, Davidic dynasty). The promise is God's coming to his people; the many promises are manifestations or illustrations of the effectiveness of his coming *to save* or *to judge*, for that is the nature of his Word.

But there is more! The crucial role of promise and promises in the Old Testament shows that the Old Testament witnesses are always pointing toward the future. When one promise or one set of promises is fulfilled, they look forward to his coming again. When David set up the monarchy, an entire block of promises had

3. See Walther Zimmerli, "Promise and Fulfillment" in *Essays on Old Testament Hermeneutics,* ed. Claus Westermann; Eng. ed. James Luther Mays (Richmond, Va.: John Knox Press, 1963), p. 105.

been fulfilled: the people had become a nation, then had received the land; they had experienced rest! But the activity of God immediately pointed forward to new promises: an enduring dynasty and a temple. When the kings of that dynasty gave the people little comfort or consolation, God pointed to a new promise: that he would set up his own kingdom and establish in it an ideal king of the Davidic line. There is constantly a future element in the promise of God, and so the definition should be expanded: *the promise is of God himself whose faithful activity with his people constantly points forward to a future coming which ultimately will be decisive not only for the people of Israel but for the whole world as well.* It is this future eschatological deed which is proclaimed in such places as Isaiah 65–66, in Zechariah 9 and 14, and elsewhere.

In this sense, it seems, Christians can look at God's deed in Christ as the fulfillment of the Old Testament promise, for that promise is of him who comes, and in Jesus Christ he came decisively for all the world. In the eschatological deed in Jesus Christ, God brought the history of his coming to its goal (*telos*). Granted, the definition does not come directly out of the Old Testament; it comes to formulation in the eyes of one who considers the Christ event to be not isolated but the climax to God's prior activity with his people Israel. This constant faithful activity is *"the* promise."

Now there are two observations to be made concerning this understanding of the promise.

First, the promise cannot be equated either with law or gospel alone, for when God comes in his Word, he may come to his people to judge with the law or to save with the gospel or to accomplish both simultaneously. God's promise may take the form of threat and judgment, of wrath and disaster, as well as of redemption and grace, of kindness and mercy. For when God comes to be with his people, there is no way to determine in advance what effect his Word will have. When Isaiah went into the temple to worship his God, he had no hint that God would drive him to his knees confessing, "Woe is me! For I am lost; for I am a man of unclean lips, and I dwell in the midst of a people of unclean lips; for my eyes have seen the King, the Lord of hosts!" (Isa. 6:5). When Job argued for almost forty chapters to have an out-and-out legal dispute with God so that he could prove his innocence, he had no idea that he too would end up on his knees crying, "I had heard of thee by the hearing of the ear, but now my eye sees thee; therefore, I despise myself, and repent in dust and ashes!" (Job 42:5–6). That is the *promise as law*! But when God comes to forgive the people who made the golden calf, when he delivers his people from bondage from Egypt and from Babylon, when he points them beyond themselves to a blessing for all mankind—that may indeed be the gospel promised which is fulfilled in Jesus the Christ (cf. Gal. 3:8).

Second, if the many promises in the Old Testament are illustrations or manifestations of the promise of God's faithful activity which points toward a future decisive act, then those Old Testament passages must be allowed to speak for themselves. That is, even though we regard that future decisive act to be fulfilled in Christ, we cannot read Christ into the many promises beforehand. If the activity of God in the Old Testament is the confrontation of his promised Word, i.e., of himself, then we ought to allow that text to speak the Word without reading into a passage what it did not contain originally. To be sure, even in some of these promises or acts of God witnessed to in the Old Testament, we must see Christ the *corrective* at work! For the witnesses at times may have allowed a nationalistic or otherwise distorted view to influence their testimony to the promise. But if exegesis of the text demonstrates a witness to the Yahweh whom we know as the Father of Jesus Christ, then let that text bear its witness and proclaim the promise of the Word to us on its own ground.

This understanding of promise differs somewhat from that of Gerhard von Rad, for that scholar applies a form of typology to the Old Testament texts and finds them saying something about Christ—although that "shadow" or "prefiguration" may not have been present in the mind of the original author or audience. For von Rad, each expression of the promise, i.e., each of the promises, contains a valid proclamation in itself, but it simultaneously carried a hint toward God's eschatological deed in Christ, and so each dealing of God in history may already be a Christ-event.[4] From

---

4. Gerhard von Rad, "Typological Interpretation of the Old Testament" in *Essays on Old Testament Hermeneutics*, p. 39. For a more complete presentation of von Rad's view see his *Old Testament Theology*, vol. 2, trans. D. M. G. Stalker (New York: Harper & Row, 1965), pp. 319–409.

the present writer's point of view, what points to a decisive event (which we recognize to be the Christ event) is *the* promise of God's faithful activity. Each expression of this promise in individual acts does not prefigure Christ, point mysteriously to him, for each of the promises is itself a proclamation of the Word. In other words, an Old Testament event (*a* promise) may contain its own end in itself; it does not have to point beyond itself to Christ. The gift of land, the exodus deliverance, the election of Zion—these are promises which result from *the* promise, but they do not themselves prefigure Christ. To be sure, some of these events may be *typical* of the way God acts in the New Testament, and in that sense Christians can preach on some of them. However, we do not have to set beside the Old Testament passage a New Testament one in order to make it valid for proclamation; nor do we have to see that Old Testament passage as pointing to Jesus Christ in a prefigurative sense to make it preachable.

This is not to say that nothing in the Old Testament points to the decisive event of the future, for there are many promises in the Old Testament which do not result in God's fulfillment in the Old Testament period: the Messiah, the kingdom of God, the universal blessing, the new covenant, etc. All these promises continue the promise of his coming, and all point to something decisive, something beyond the reality of the situation out of which they came. In these cases, in other words, *the* promise points to a future act.

What we must be careful to avoid, therefore, is forcing the future into the Old Testament's present activity of God. Both the future promises and the present acts of God are expressions of *the* promise, namely, God's faithful activity. But from this point of view, the future is not to be read into every act of God. Or, to use the typology of von Rad, every act of God in Israel's history does not hint at, prefigure the Christ event. This is not to say that the acts of God in the Old Testament are a helter-skelter mess which go nowhere; for the journey is indeed from promise to fulfillment. It is simply to say that an individual act of God in the Old Testament may be considered in itself proclamation of the Word of God without seeing it point to the future. The Old Testament text must speak for itself. When it does, it may or may not be valid for the Christian proclaimer, and that is the point at which our Christian presuppositions take seriously the direction from New Testament to Old Testament, from fulfillment to promise, from radical correction to sometimes distorted witness.

THE CHRISTIAN IN THE PROMISE-FULFILLMENT TENSION

The Christian stands in the age of fulfillment, the era of the New Testament, the new time. He is part of the new Israel, the end of days, the final moment. He is the church which is called and gathered by and through God's act in Christ. That act has ultimate significance; it is the goal of God's activity; it is the *telos*, the fulfillment of his promise. It is an eschatological act! Or better, it is *the* eschatological act which ushers in the eschatological kingdom, which calls the eschatological people of God, the church. In other words, the future is here.

In the area of astrology there is debate as to whether the future has already begun, for while some astrologers argue that the age of Aquarius has already dawned, others say that it will not begin until the new millennium at 2000. In the area of technology we are never certain where we are because, while some talk about what is possible for the future, others are already working on, or in fact accomplishing, some of those "future" possibilities. But in the arena of Christian theology the future is already upon us, for we live *now* in the new age ushered in by God's redemptive act in Christ. For the church the future is now! The old aeon has been replaced by the new; the kingdom of God is upon us! B.C. time is gone, and A.D. time is here! Believers are already redeemed from the present evil aeon (Gal. 1:4) and already taste the powers of the future aeon (Heb. 6:5). Moreover, if the resurrection of the dead implies the transition from the one aeon to the other and the beginning of the new and eternal creation, then the new aeon has already begun in and with the resurrection of Christ, for this event is the beginning of the general resurrection, the first fruits of those who have fallen asleep (1 Cor. 15:20, 23).

Having said all that, we may argue that the old aeon is putting up a good fight to stay alive. While the new aeon is here, it is not yet fully consummated, and so the old aeon, like the dragon thrown down by Michael (Rev. 12:7 ff.), is literally "raising hell" because he knows that his time is short. Therefore the church looks to the future, comforted by the promise that all things will be made new, that evil power will cease to exist, that all men will have new bodies which feel no pain, no hunger, no weariness, no discrimination in regard to skin pigmentation.

Thus the future is already here but not yet fully consummated. And so the church, while looking back to God's act of fulfillment in Christ, simultaneously lives under the promise that God will send Christ again to make all things new. For that reason, though the church is the New Testament people of God created by his act in Jesus Christ, Christians are in some sense Old Testament men inasmuch as we live in a time of promise. It is true that in the Old Testament there is a looking backward, especially to the Exodus event. But equally prominent is the forward-looking witness to some future activity of God—sometimes immediate future and other times distant future. This Janus-type witness is clear in the New Testament as well, for while the witnesses look back to the life, death, and resurrection of Christ, they simultaneously point to his constant coming and to his second advent when the new age will be completely consummated.

Thus, standing where we do, we live in the confusing time which is both promise and fulfillment—in the time of God's faithful activity which has passed the decisive moment but which still looks forward to a final consummation. The church is thus a community of the future inasmuch as it already is what it shall be, and yet it is not fully what it shall be when faith passes over into sight.

Now if New Testament man lives like Old Testament man, under the promise of God's faithful activity, wherein is the difference or the uniqueness of the New Testament? The uniqueness of the Christian under promise can only be discussed in terms of the uniqueness of the *fulfillment,* and there are several issues crucial in this regard.

The fulfillment in the Christ-event is, first of all, an act of God to reconcile the world to himself—an act which happened in time and space and which has once and for all significance. It is an act which far transcends our own existential situation, for it is effective for man and is not dependent on our comprehension of it. To be sure, it makes a difference in our lives only when we are confronted by the news of it, only when we are seized by the God who performed it. But its effectiveness for the world is not dependent upon our understanding. This act of reconciliation need never be repeated. It must be proclaimed, but it can never be done again, and it need never be done again. God's act in Christ has accomplished reconciliation; it has once and for all won the victory over the power of sin. There is no act in the Old Testament which can make such a claim. In the Old Testament God forgives sins and even provides the means—cultic persons, sacrifice, etc.—in order to accomplish this forgiveness of sins. But in the Old Testament there is no real understanding of *sin* as that which has control of us; there is no real understanding of *sinner* as that which we are by our very being. In the Old Testament there are sins which men commit, and for which men need forgiveness, but these are acts of commission and omission which can be avoided if men had the will to do so. Now without the New Testament depth of sin, there is likewise lacking in the Old Testament the depth of forgiveness which is manifested in the New Testament by the fact that God came to die for sinners.

The forgiveness of sin, the reconciliation of the world to God —all this in the New Testament is accomplished through the *person* of Jesus Christ. This is unique for New Testament man, for it is now this Christ who is the way, the truth, and the life. It is in relationship with God through Christ that we experience forgiveness, that we encounter the promise of God's faithfulness, and that we know and praise the Father. Moreover, it is the person of Christ who is the object not only of our gratitude for his sacrifice, but who is the object of our worship and praise as well. He is not only the one in whom God effected salvation; he is also the Lord whom we worship and praise. He is not one who is simply the man for others; he is the one who is Lord of the world.

Thus, Christians live under the promise that this Christ who died on a cross and was raised from the dead will come again— daily when *he* is proclaimed, and ultimately to consummate the eschatological day which he has already inaugurated. Thus the promise for us is not identical to that of the Old Testament. To be sure, *the* promise of God's faithful activity continues; it continues because the final consummation is yet to occur. The promise is thus like or similar to that of the Old Testament. But it is not identical because (1) the promise for us of God's coming is in terms of the person of Christ and (2) the promise for us runs parallel to the fulfillment in which God has already reconciled the world to himself. In other words, what is unique about the Christian under the promise is precisely the fact that the Christian is simultaneously under the fulfillment of God in the *person and work of Christ.*

Now the uniqueness of the New Testament or of the Christian under the promise-fulfillment tension does not invalidate the Old Testament witness to the promise. It does mean, however, that there will be a difference in the way the Christian understands the Old Testament promise. While forgiveness of sins in the Old Testament does not include the depth of the New Testament understanding or the person of Christ as the Redeemer, nevertheless the Christian who *knows* that person and work of Christ will understand more deeply those passages in the Old Testament which speak of sins and which proclaim God's forgiveness—and perhaps he will be able to proclaim the Word of God on the basis of the Old Testament texts. The Christian who knows the fulfillment in Christ may see a depth of understanding in the Old Testament texts which proclaim that God comes to guide his people; to give them direction in bewildering times; to set them loose on a mission; to release them from the confining bonds of imprisonment, slavery, exile, persecution; to judge his people for failing to do justice and for forsaking him for idols; to drive men to their knees by his mere presence. All these events do not point typologically to Christ, i.e., prefigure him, hint at him, give a shadow of him. Rather Christ points the Christian to those texts which proclaim these promises of God, and in this pointing gives them a depth of meaning they could not originally have had because the authors or the audience did not know the fulfillment of God's promise! They did not know God as we do—as the one who came to die on our behalf; they did not know sin as we do—as such a powerful evil that God in Christ had to die in order to overcome it; they did not know reconciliation as we do—that God has acted to redeem us once and for all. Thus those Old Testament texts which proclaim God's coming to judge and to save, to comfort and to challenge, are filled for the Christian with new meaning, for

Christ points us back to the promise which he both fulfills and corrects.

That Christ points us back to Old Testament texts to correct them may mean, of course, that some are so corrected that they do not and cannot proclaim the Word of the God as we know it through God's revelation in his Son. Many proverbs leave much to be desired from the Christian perspective; they represent in large measure typical ancient wisdom. Much of the Book of Job, especially where the friends of Job proclaim optimistic wisdom (the good are rewarded; the wicked are punished), lies outside the realm of Christian proclamation. The slaughter of the firstborn of Egypt portrays a God who seems to have no relationship to the Father of Jesus Christ. And there is much material that is simply irrelevant for the Christian, especially cultic ordinances and ritual laws. The canon within the canon principle must be taken seriously if Christ is not only the fulfillment of the Old Testament promise but also the corrective to some of the testimony to the God of that promise. One must, therefore, be selective in choosing what is appropriate in order to proclaim the Word of God, and this proclamation from an Old Testament text may result in gospel or in law for those confronted by him who comes in his Word.

Chapter Four:

Proclaiming the God

of the Promise

A CONCERN FOR HISTORICITY

The biblical witnesses testify that God's Word confronts man *in history*, i.e., that the time-and-space-bound arena of history is where the Word of Yahweh meets man and where it is manifested in terms of the unfolding of his will. Without this concern for history there stands the danger of dissolving the Word of God into a timeless myth. The first implication of that concern, however, is the importance of the historicity of the event, i.e., what actually happened. Such a quest, to be sure, involves immediate problems, because the resources at our disposal are extremely limited, and because often the limited resources conflict in their reporting of the incident. For example, the scarcity of material available to determine precisely "what happened" at the Reed Sea (Exodus 14–15) is inded frustrating, for while the event is recorded by a number of sources—to say nothing of the little historical summaries of Josh. 24:2–13 and Psalms 105, 106, 135, 136—there is no extra-biblical material to substantiate any of these somewhat diverse reports. To have some mention of the incident in Egyptian records would certainly be a help, but perhaps it would be too much to expect an ancient army to record its losing an encounter by getting stuck in the mud. On the other hand, in the case of Sennacherib's siege of Jerusalem due to the political maneuvering of Hezekiah (Isaiah 36–37, 2 Kings 18–19, 2 Chron. 32:1–21) we do have an extra-biblical account in the records of Sennacherib himself. However, while the biblical records proclaim that Sennacherib's siege failed because of the plague brought about by the Lord's angel (2 Kings 19:35, 36; 2 Chron. 32:20–23; Isa. 38:36–38), Sennacherib claims that he brought the city to its knees and locked up Hezekiah "like a bird in a cage" (which may reflect the little incident at 2 Kings 18:13–16). Thus, even where more evidence is available, it is often contradictory, and thus "what happened" becomes even more of a mystery.

But in spite of the difficulties of available and even contradictory source material, the quest for what happened must continue, for without this concern for the historical setting, there is no situation to which the Word is addressed, and there is no concreteness to the testimony. It must always be borne in mind, then, that when an exegete interprets the situation of the text, he speaks only on the basis of what evidence is available and makes a judgment only on the basis of what is *probable*. But he must at least consider the possibility of the occurrence and attempt to understand that occurrence as accurately as possible. Yahweh of the Old Testament who is the Father of Jesus Christ does break into time and space situations, and so those situations must be seriously considered! Therefore a knowledge of Israel's history within her ancient Near Eastern environment is not a luxury but is as necessary a tool for the interpretation of the Old Testament as the history of the first century A.D. is for the New.

THE HISTORY OF THE WORD OF GOD

As necessary as this concern for historicity is, historicity does not proclaim anyone; what happened must be interpreted as the act of God as he operates between promise and fulfillment. In other words, God confronts us not in the historicity of the biblical event but in the Word which is proclaimed through the biblical witness. It is the proclaimed Word of God out of the biblical text that is the means by which God comes to be present now—to judge and to save, to comfort and to challenge. God addresses men through the words and proclamation of other men.

If that is so, then it is not absolutely essential that every biblical text describe an incident which actually happened. To fail to find the historicity of a passage or to discover that such a passage is an old literary piece—a legend, a saga, or a myth—does not invalidate the message of the text. For while we might attempt to allow the possibility that such a thing happened, we may discover that it is most unlikely that there was an occurrence behind it. The concern for historicity is basically to keep the witness of the Bible down to earth, to show that God breaks into history, that the coming of the transcendent God into our midst is typical of the same God who came in Christ to die for our sakes. But since the Word proclaimed is the significant event for man, then whether or not everything actually happened is not crucial. What is crucial is whether that proclamation is based upon and consistent with the God who confronts man in history by his Word become flesh and who by that confrontation event creates history anew.

Thus, we speak of the history of the Word of God, i.e., the history of God breaking into the world through proclamation, working to fulfill the promise of his faithful activity. In this sense we do not intend to describe a salvation history which logically results in the Christ-event as though there could be no other possibility once the Old Testament was finally written, a salvation history which piles up bigger and bigger promises until Christ comes as the biggest promise. Rather God's promise of blessing to be bestowed on all men comes to fulfillment (and correction) in Christ, and that fulfillment does not necessarily depend upon an evolutionary scheme which moves from the exodus event to the Davidic covenant to the indestructibility of Zion and to all other promises. To put it in positive terms, God's promise of a decisive coming for man is what is fulfilled in the Christ event. Until that event God's promise takes the form of his election of a people and his faithful activity among them. But out of any of these activities or out of the sum total of these activities, the Christ event does not evolve naturally, and so he need not be read into them. However, in the witness to many of these acts, the God who came decisively in Christ may encounter us, and so such texts might be quite useful in Christian preaching. Thus, the Christian interpreter must, on the basis of what a text meant, decide what it means for Christians wherever they are and at what moment in time.[1]

INTERPRETATION AS PROCLAMATION

It has already been said that even in the texts for which much historical evidence is available and even when the historical situation can be worked out rather precisely, the Word of God is not proclaimed by simply setting forth "what happened." If the theory could be finally confirmed that Sennacherib's army besieging Jerusalem became ill and had to return to Assyria in 701 and that the takeover of the city by Assyrians really describes an incident which took place during a second siege some twelve years later, that theory says nothing which can be classified as proclamation. It is only when the incident is interpreted as the act of Yahweh that the event takes on theological significance. In the case of the story about the siege of Jerusalem, only when the story can be summed up by saying, "Yahweh responds to his people who wait in faith by fulfilling his promise that Jerusalem/Zion is indestructible," that the story becomes proclamation of the God of the promise. In the case of the exodus event at Exodus 14, while the historical situation cannot be determined precisely and in detail, it seems that something significant occurred there which enabled a later interpreter to say, "Yahweh redeems his people from a bondage from which they are unable and even unwilling to save themselves." This interpretation is proclamation of the faithful activity of God with his people.

The examples just cited demonstrate that it is not any interpretation which is proclamation, for obviously historical incidents can be interpreted in a variety of ways. It is only when the interpretation offers an answer to the question "What is God doing here?" that the text proclaims *the* promise of God, the sending of his

---

1. This distinction between what a text meant and what it means has been made most sharply by Krister Stendahl in "Biblical Theology, Contemporary," *Interpreter's Dictionary of the Bible* (Nashville: Abingdon Press, 1962), vol. I, pp. 418–432. For Stendahl, however, this distinction has become a separation in which the biblical exegete does not have any responsibility to move beyond what it meant; what the text means is someone else's responsibility.

Word, the activity of God with his people. If that question is asked of a text, then it must be answered by the present interpreter with a statement of which God is the subject. That is, after all the exegetical work is done, one must ask the question "What is God doing here?" and then answer it according to that text's proclamation: "God is . . . ." In that way the interpreter cannot end up giving a morality speech or encouraging works righteousness or giving a lecture about the passage. One is forced to deal with God and his promise.

At the same time, if the promise of God is understood as his faithful activity with his people, then the situation in which God comes to be present is essential to the theology of the text. The God of the Bible is not presented in philosophical absolutes or in a historical vacuum. Therefore, theological interpretation of a text must include the situation(s) of the people to whom God comes in his Word. When one asks of a text "What is God doing *here?*" then the situation or the problem of the situation must be included in the statement which answers the question with God as the subject. To announce that "God redeems his people" is to speak correctly, but such an announcement permits great distortion of a given text and, in fact, could be proclaimed from hundreds of texts without any exegesis at all. But when one works through Exodus 14 to answer, "Yahweh redeems his people from a bondage from which they are unable and even unwilling to save themselves," then the interpreter does justice to the dynamic God of the Bible who acts and speaks anew in each new concrete situation.

TEXTUAL AND CONTEXTUAL PREACHING

1. WHAT THE TEXT MEANT

To determine the significance of a given pericope or book in the Scriptures, the exegete is compelled to use all the scientific tools and methods at his disposal. In one sense, the Bible is a historical document (or rather, a collection of documents) and must be examined like any other historical document. At the same time, the Bible is that collection of witness literature which provides the norm for our faith as Christians. And so, unlike other historical documents, we approach the study of the Bible with some commitments to the God to whom it bears witness and with some presuppositions concerning its nature. Carrying such presuppositions and commitments, one's exegesis will not be completely objective. One's understanding of the Word of God and of inspiration cannot, and should not, be divorced from the task of determining what the text meant. Even one's purpose for examining the Scriptures is, of course, based on some presupposition which will undoubtedly influence what one finds.

The position previously set forth in this volume is that the Word of God is the means by which God confronts man in time and space and by which God effects his will. Such a position, true of the Old Testament as well as the New, where this Word became flesh, means that one cannot define in absolute terms precisely what the Word of God says. For if God is understood as the one who faithfully comes to his people to judge and to save, then his Word always has a message for a particular situation, and the content and structure of that Word is always determined by the situation which God addresses. When the Word of the Lord comes to a prophet, there always follows a specific message to be spoken to a particular people at a certain point in time. That this Word is no theological, philosophical, or moral absolute but the dynamic confrontation of God with man is both a commitment and a presupposition which will undoubtedly have some influence on one's understanding of what the text meant.

As for the matter of inspiration, the position or presupposition in the present writer's understanding is that we would have no Bible if God had not inspired men to bear witness to him, to be his spokesmen. Moreover, the witness which these inspired men gave have the power to call others to salvation. The preceding chapters, however, should have made clear already that it is the men of the Bible who were inspired, and that the expressions—even of inspired men—remain nevertheless human testimony which is always influenced by and limited to man's comprehension of the will of God in relation to the contemporary situation. Thus the words which these inspired men used are subject to the closest scrutiny we can devise. Only with such examination can we begin to interpret what the text meant.

Taking seriously such presuppositions and commitments, the

interpreter approaches the texts of Scripture with all the tools and methods at his disposal.[2] The steps for exegesis outlined here differ very little from other such lists, although the theological and hermeneutical position of the present writer will cause certain aspects of the list to be emphasized more than others. In addition, since the concern here is with exegesis of Old Testament texts in particular, the emphasis on some items in the list will be somewhat different from a list concerned with New Testament interpretation.

a. Establish a working text. The ideal method of establishing the text is, of course, to translate it from the Hebrew—and to render it as literally as possible. (The literal translation will prevent the exegete from making an interpretative rendering before

2. Books, articles, and reports of commissions concerning methods of biblical study abound today. For a summary of this work among Roman Catholics and Protestants, as well as a concise presentation of his own outline, see John Reumann, "Methods in Studying the Biblical Text Today," *Concordia Theological Monthly* 40 (1969), pp. 655–681. Dr. Reumann acknowledges a theological influence from Gerhard Ebeling and Heinrich Ott and a terminological one from a volume by Otto Kaiser and W. G. Kümmel, *Exegetical Method: A Student's Handbook*, trans. E. V. N. Goetchius (New York: Seabury Press, 1967).

Among the many tools available in English are Bible dictionaries, notably *The Interpreter's Dictionary of the Bible*, 4 vols. (Nashville: Abington Press, 1962) and above all, *Theological Dictionary of the New Testament*, eds. Gerhard Kittel and Gerhard Friedrich; Eng. trans. and ed. Geoffrey W. Bromiley (Grand Rapids, Mich.: William B. Eerdmans, 1964–); concordances such as Robert Young's *Analytical Concordance to the Bible* (Grand Rapids, Mich.: William B. Eerdmans, rev. ed., 1970) and *Nelson's Complete Concordance of the Revised Standard Version Bible* (New York: Nelson & Sons, 1957), as well as Bible atlases, histories of Israel, general introductions, and, of course, commentaries. Two useful one-volume commentaries on the Bible are *The Interpreter's One Volume Commentary on the Bible*, ed. Charles M. Laymon (Nashville: Abingdon Press, 1971), and *Peake's Commentary on the Bible*, ed. Matthew Black, rev. ed. (London: Thomas Nelson & Sons, 1962). While each commentary should be examined on its own merit, as a series in Old Testament books the "Old Testament Library" volumes published by Westminster Press are particularly good as theological works, as are those in the "Hermeneia" series now being published by Fortress Press. Especially helpful as a complete list and description of the use of such tools is Frederick W. Danker's *Multipurpose Tools for Bible Study*, 3d rev. ed. (St. Louis: Concordia Publishing House, 1970).

Valuable as introductions to the various "criticisms" in biblical exegesis are the concise volumes in Fortress Press's "Guides to Biblical Scholarship." The New Testament Series includes Norman Perrin's *What Is Redaction Criticism?* (1969); Edgar V. McKnight's *What Is Form Criticism?* (1969); William A. Beardslee's *Literary Criticism of the New Testament* (1970); and William G. Doty's *Letters in Primitive Christianity* (1973). The Old Testament Series includes Norman Habel's *Literary Criticism of the Old Testament* (1971); Gene M. Tucker's *Form Criticism of the Old Testament* (1971); and Walter E. Rast's *Tradition History and the Old Testament* (1972). These volumes are highly recommended for those who are unclear about the nature and methods of these aspects of biblical study. *Textual Criticism of the Old Testament* by Ralph W. Klein is to appear in the same series in 1974.

the hard work of exegesis has begun.) Fortunately or unfortunately, the exegete of an Old Testament text does not need to expend as much time and energy in establishing the Hebrew text as the New Testament exegete must do with the Greek. This difference is due simply to the fact that we do not possess variant ancient Hebrew manuscripts apart from the limited and often fragmented texts from the Dead Sea community at Qumran.[3]

For those unable to translate the text from Hebrew, another method of establishing a working text is available, namely, by comparing various English translations or paying attention to footnotes in most translations to see if any significant differences appear. The simple use of synonyms is unimportant, but the different rendering of an idiom, the use or lack of use of an article, the tense or mood of a verb—any of these might at least hint at a problem. For example, at Isa. 7:14 the *Authorized Version* reads, "Behold, a virgin shall conceive, and bear a son, . . ."; the *Revised Standard Version* renders the same verse as "Behold, a young woman shall conceive and bear a son, . . ."; the *New English Bible*, "A young woman is with child, and she will bear a son, . . ."; and in his recent commentary Otto Kaiser translates, "if a young woman, who is now pregnant, bear a son, . . ."[4] The significance of the different translations is obvious—both in terms of the identity of the woman and of the child and the time of conception.[5] However, since the final translation on which the exegete decides will depend on further investigation, such differences should simply be noted at this stage.

b. Work through literary matters. The literary aspects of a text are many and varied—in fact, almost infinite. The major concerns, however, are as follows:

1. The author, his date, and his purpose for writing or speaking. To determine the probable answers to these issues, the inter-

---

3. Where such Dead Sea texts are available and where variations from the received text occur, the editors of Kittel's *Biblia Hebraica* have included a third paragraph in the apparatus at the bottom of the page on which the text appears. For those gifted in languages, the Septuagint can sometimes serve as an aid in establishing the text, for one can sometimes determine the Hebrew reading which the Greek translator had before him.

4. Otto Kaiser, *Isaiah 1–12*, trans. R. A. Wilson, "The Old Testament Library" (Philadelphia: Westminster Press, 1972), p. 96.

5. It is interesting that none of the above translations renders the Hebrew literally: "Behold *the* young woman is with child. . . ."

preter should use a sound and relatively recent Old Testament introduction, or a commentary by a reputable scholar, if such is available on the book in which the passage occurs.[6]

2. Literary devices and laws of composition. Is the passage prose or poetry? If poetry, does it follow the rules and patterns for parallelism? If so, which kind of parallelism—synonymous, antithetic, climbing? If synonymous, then two lines of poetry—by the use of synonyms—mean the same thing. Such a discovery can prevent serious distortion of a text. For example, at Isa. 55:7 appears the synonymous parallelism:

"let the wicked forsake his way,
  and the unrighteous man his thoughts;
let him return to the Lord, that he may have
  mercy on him,
and to our God, for he will abundantly pardon."

It might be tempting to separate the wicked man's way from the unrighteous man's thoughts and to distinguish between the Lord's mercy and God's pardon. Such divisions may indeed be tempting in a sermon outline, but the text intends no such differentiation between lines one and two and between lines three and four. If the passage under investigation is prose, are there any important and typically narrative-type expressions which stand out? The famous Immanuel passage at Isa. 7:10–17 begins, "Again the Lord spoke to Ahaz. . . ." The simple adverb "again" obviously indicates that he had spoken earlier, and that prior conversation in 7:1–9 might be crucial in interpreting the present one.

3. Key words and idioms. The presence of typical theological terms such as righteousness, salvation, transgression, iniquity, and redeem deserves attention. One way to grasp what the biblical writers meant by such terms is to use a Bible dictionary. Another way, open both to those who can read Hebrew and those who cannot, is to do a word study through the use of a concordance. Using a

---

6. Especially commendable as introductions to the Old Testament are Otto Eissfeldt, *The Old Testament: An Introduction*, trans. P. R. Ackroyd (New York: Harper & Row, 1965); Georg Fohrer, *Introduction to the Old Testament*, trans. David E. Green (Nashville: Abington Press, 1968); and Arthur Weiser, *The Old Testament: Its Formation and Development*, trans. Dorothea M. Barton (New York: Association Press, 1961).

Hebrew concordance or an English one, however, requires some caution. The purpose of such word studies is, of course, to make some conclusion about the meaning of the word to Old Testament people on the basis of how and in what contexts the word is used. But since the meanings of words change and since different authors use words in somewhat different ways, it is important to establish a set of priorities in carrying out such a study. First, how is the word used elsewhere by the same author? Second, how is the word used by the author's contemporaries? Third, how is the word used generally in the Old Testament? The further down in this list the interpreter must move in order to acquire enough evidence to make some conclusion about the use of a word, the less precise he will be in making a judgment on the passage under investigation. If a certain author nowhere else used the term in question and if none of his contemporaries used the word, then the greatest of caution must be exercised in determining precisely what the author meant on the basis of word usage at his time. To illustrate this point, let us consider the word *subdue* at Gen. 1:28 which, of course, has such profound significance in modern discussions on ecology. A word study of Hebrew *kbs* or the English word *subdue* reveals precisely what we would not want it to mean: to enslave, to oppress, to bring into bondage. The contexts in which the word appears give an entirely negative sense to the word. However, there is not one other instance in which the author of Genesis 1—the Priestly writer—uses the term, and so the interpreter must be extremely careful in concluding that the Priest meant "subdue" in a negative sense, especially since he speaks so positively about the created world throughout the chapter.

Key words, of course, are sometimes the problematical ones discovered in establishing the text, and so at this point of the process, the exegete should try to determine whether Isa. 7:14 should read "A virgin shall conceive" or "A young woman is with child." Such a problem involves a word study of the term for the female (Hebrew *'almāh*) as well as the use of a good commentary which should discuss the verb as a present participle or as a simple adjective.

The investigation of idioms is crucial at this stage. Sometimes idioms are difficult to recognize as such, but often they stand out prominently. When one reads in the Aaronic benediction, "The Lord make his face to shine upon you" (Num. 6:25), he is obviously dealing with an idiom. A word study of "shine" in connection with one's face shows that the idiom stands in synonymous parallelism with "save" (Ps. 31:16), "be gracious" (Ps. 67:1), "restore" (Ps. 80:3, 7, 19), and "redeem" (Ps. 119:134–135). Since the benediction of Numbers 6 and the psalms obviously have a common cultic setting, the meaning of the idiom is rather clear.

c. Determine the situation in life. The so-called *Sitz im Leben* involves an inquiry into the situation in which a given proclamation was issued. This "setting in life" includes, first of all, the historical events of the time of the author or authors of a text, for how can the preaching of Isaiah be understood apart from the Assyrian and other threats against Judah in the second half of the eighth century B.C.? What meaning has the preaching of Second Isaiah apart from the long exile in Babylon? To repeat what was said earlier, the Word of God in the Bible always addresses particular situations, and so those situations in history are crucial to the interpretation of a passage.

At the same time, the "situation in life" includes more than the sequence of events in Israel or in the ancient Near East. It involves as well social, psychological, cultural, and economic factors. The willingness of Lot to give his virgin daughters to the mob at his door rather than surrender his guests (Gen. 19:1–11) is incomprehensible apart from the ancient rules of hospitality. The Philistines' guilt offering of five golden tumors and five golden mice (1 Sam. 6:1–5) is simply humorous apart from the ancient magical belief that one could ward off the evil effects of a disaster by making a replica of it. Such elements of a life's situation are usually described in a good commentary or in such a volume as Theodor H. Gaster's *Myth, Legend, and Custom in the Old Testament*.[7]

The determination of the setting to and in which the Word of God was proclaimed by the Yahwist, Isaiah, or the Priest leads immediately and directly to the question of the theological implica-

---

7. Theodor H. Gaster, *Myth, Legend, and Custom in the Old Testament* (New York: Harper & Row, 1969).

tions of that situation. When Ahaz stood in danger of losing his throne to Rezin of Damascus as a result of the Syro-Ephraimite alliance (Isa. 7:1–9), the theological problem at stake was the credibility of Yahweh's promise that a Davidic king would always sit on Jerusalem's throne (2 Sam. 7). When the people of Judah were carried off as exiles into Babylon, the theological difficulties which the Deuteronomists, Ezekiel, and Second Isaiah had to address were: What happened to God's promise of the indestructibility of Zion? Has God called off the covenant relationship in which he promised to protect us? If so, why? Is God alive now that his temple where he lived and the Ark on which he sat as king have gone up in smoke? How can God, if he is alive, be reached when exiles in Babylon have no means of traveling to his sanctuaries in Israel? The struggling with such questions was the reason that many biblical writings were preserved. If the historical situation is at all related to the preaching of the Word, then the modern interpreter must try to determine the theological problem of the given situation to which a theological answer was preached.

d. Employ the criticisms (form, source, redaction, and tradition). While full descriptions of the nature and methods of these disciplines are readily accessible,[8] brief descriptions of each are presented here in order to emphasize the usefulness of these disciplines for preaching from Old Testament text.

1. *Form criticism* involves the task of classifying a passage on the basis of its structure and content. Usually the concern is with the oral or pre-literary stage of the unit, but form criticism also applies to written documents. As is the case with a business letter, a sonnet, or a limerick today, so ancient people used prescibed forms for oral and written communication. The desired form was determined, as today, by the use it was intended to serve. Thus, a cultic, a legal, a sermonic, or a story-telling function determined which set of forms was to be used. There have been described an infinite number of prose and a likewise staggering list of poetic forms in the Old Testament—forms which contain common sets of characteristics which modern interpreters label as sagas, legends,

---

8. See the series "Guides to Biblical Scholarship" cited above in note 2.

announcements of salvation and of judgment, psalms of lament, etc.[9]

Such identification of forms enables the interpreter to compare and contrast other uses of the same form in order to see which aspects of a pericope are simply typical of the way something was said or written, and which elements stand out as being different—and thus perhaps crucial to its use. For example, if one compares the reports of prophetic calls at Isa. 6:1–13; Jer. 1:4–10; and Ezek. 2:1–3:16, one discovers some common expressions as well as a basic structure. In addition, the intended purpose of each of these accounts is the same: to provide some validity or authenticity for the preaching of these men as messengers of Yahweh. At the same time, some obvious differences are present in these reports which, precisely because they are different, may enable the interpreter to discern an emphasis intended by the original reporter or by the composer of the piece as we have it. In Isaiah's call the event takes place in the Jerusalem Temple, and the report includes the forgiveness of Isaiah's sins. These features are not present in the reports concerning Jeremiah and Ezekiel. When the Lord asks for a volunteer to be his spokesman, Isaiah responds immediately; when Jeremiah is confronted by the Lord with his designated task, this prophet-to-be offers some excuses (like Moses at Exod. 3:11; 4:10) in order to avoid the task; Ezekiel does not respond at all in words but obeys the instructions given to him. Thus, the common features and purpose of the three reports are balanced by the particular emphasis of each—all of which should be noted.

When using a psalm or part of a psalm as a text for preaching or as part of the liturgy, form criticism plays an important role. A commentary of recent vintage will help determine the type of a given psalm and thus give a clue concerning its use in Israel's wor-

9. While forms have been described and identified for every book and for every kind of literature in the Old Testament, some basic descriptions in several areas are readily available in English. The pioneer in this discipline, Hermann Gunkel, did most of his work in the narratives of Genesis and in the Book of Psalms. His methods and concerns, while now somewhat refined and modified, are readily available in English in *The Psalms*, trans. Thomas M. Horner, "Facet Books—Biblical Series, 19" (Philadelphia: Fortress Press, 1967), and *The Legends of Genesis*, trans. W. H. Caruth (New York: Schocken Books, 1964). In prophetic literature, especially commendable is Claus Westermann's *Basic Forms of Prophetic Speech*, trans. H. C. White (Philadelphia: Wesminster Press, 1967).

ship life. To determine that a psalm is a community lament might be significant in its use in a contemporary setting; the same is true of a hymn or a thanksgiving or any number of possibilities. Likewise, to recognize that some psalms (such as 2 and 110) were used as part of the ceremony when a king was crowned on the Jerusalem throne might severely limit their use in our liturgies. However, even such psalms might proclaim a theology which is useful in some ways for Christian proclamation.

Determining the original level or form of a story can usually be accomplished only by working backward. Only by identifying, for example, characteristics of the Elohistic source in Genesis 22 (the sacrifice of Isaac), and by isolating these characteristics, can the interpreter work back to a pre-Elohistic oral narrative which seems to be a polemic against child sacrifice. Such an example forces us to move immediately to source criticism.

2. *Source criticism* is the science of identifying and separating the various strands of narrative and legal material in the first several books of the Bible. Ever since 1753 when Jean Astruc discovered two strands of narrative in the Book of Genesis, scholars have been debating how many strands of material are present and in how many books. Some scholars have argued for five sources, some of which can be discerned from Genesis through Kings; others have maintained there are essentially three sources which are interwoven in the Tetrateuch, but traces of a fourth source are present as well. The latter position seems to be the more sensible: running throughout the books of Genesis, Exodus, and Numbers (Leviticus is almost exclusively Priestly instruction) are the works of the Yahwist (known affectionately to scholars as J), the Elohist (E) and the Priest (P). The J source seems to have originated in Judah in the tenth century B.C.—at the height of David's or Solomon's glory. E is northern (Israelite) in origin, somewhat more fragmented than J, and is usually dated about 750 B.C. The Priestly material seems to have been composed in the late exilic or postexilic periods (sixth or fifth centuries B.C.) and is characterized by its use of historical narrative as the outline for the giving of cultic ordinances. The dates assigned for "origin" or "composition" are in no way conclusive for all the material contained in these sources; the

dates simply represent the approximate times in which the Yahwist, the Elohist, and the Priest did their work of collecting, editing, and organizing such material which had been handed down for centuries.

In addition to these three narrative sources which are sometimes set side by side and at other times are intertwined so delicately in the Tetrateuch, there are traces of another hand known as a Deuteronomistic editor. This school of editors/historians was active during the Babylonian exile, probably in Babylon itself, collecting, editing, and adding to many Tetrateuchal pieces as well as producing the extensive history which runs from Deuteronomy through Kings.

Each of these sources has its own typical expressions and concerns, its own ideological and theological emphases, and its own set of historical, political, and cultural situations it had to address. Whoever joined J and E together also had his own set of characteristics which are often discernible; the final compiler, probably active about 450 B.C, who gave us what is essentially the Tetrateuch as we have it, had *his* set of concerns and emphases. Thus each of the sources, as well as each of the editors, whose hands are involved in a particular story, address a new situation with a testimony to what God says to that situation. These proclamations are in addition to the proclamations of the oral stories which preceded and which were used by J, E, and P.

When J and P are separated from each other in the recording of the Reed Sea event at Exod. 14:10–31, there are present two entirely coherent and complete reports of the incident. The Yahwist's proclamation seems to be "The Lord will redeem his people if they stand still in faith," while the Priest proclaims, "In the midst of his people's conflicts Yahweh comes to prove he is Lord by showing his strength and to get glory over his enemies." When the final compiler intertwined them and included as well the murmuring motif at verses 11–12 (apparently E?), his proclamation can be summed up as "Yahweh redeems his people from a bondage from which they are unable and even unwilling to save themselves." Thus, the event at Exod. 14:10–31 contains complete reports from two stories, some isolated fragments from E, and the theological emphasis of the editor who so ingeniously intertwined them. This editorial work now leads to further discussion of redaction criticism.

3. *Redaction criticism* refers precisely to the literary editing of a passage or story in order to provide the text which we have before us. In some cases, the redactor of a passage might be the Yahwist, the Elohist, or the Priest, or the man (or men) who combined sources J and E—at some time between the work of the Elohist about 750 B.C. and the exilic period. In Tetrateuchal materials, however, the *final* redactor is the one who combined P with the already existing combination of JE (and D?). In this case the present structure of the material would have been accomplished in the post-exilic community.

The task of redaction criticism, however, involves far more than the combining and intertwining of Tetrateuchal sources. It applies as well to virtually all the literature, especially to prophetic books in which introductions to the books or to sections of the books, as well as additions to the books, are the result of the work of an individual or school in the later community. For example, it has long been recognized that the Deuteronomistic editors of the exilic period and still later editors expanded the preaching of Jeremiah. This expansion probably accounts for some of the biographical data on the prophet and for some duplications such as that of the Temple sermon at Jeremiah 7 and again in chapter 26.[10]

The determination of the work of the redactors by the use of characteristic terminology, ideology, theology, and historical circumstances enables the interpreter to see once again the continuing dynamic witness to God who addresses each generation anew. Old traditions are not cast aside; on the contrary, they are reinterpreted and reasserted by directing them to a new audience. Such redactional activity itself should guard us against regarding the final form of a passage or book as the only legitimate one for us today. The purpose of the redactor was quite the opposite of such a static representation of revelation.

4. *Tradition criticism* stands between and, in fact, includes

10. For the most recent and comprehensive study of Deuteronomistic work in Jeremiah, see E. W. Nicholson, *Preaching to the Exiles* (New York: Schocken Books, 1970).

form and redaction, for it concerns itself with the constant use and reinterpretation of traditions and/or motifs. Such reinterpretation of traditions includes, of course, the various sources of the Tetrateuch, as well as the work of the editors who combined them or added to them. The event of deliverance from Egypt is a crucial theological tradition: we have already seen that event interpreted differently by J and P; to those interpretations we added that of the redactor. But the development of this tradition reaches back to an oral period, to a poetic version in Exod. 15:1–12, and on into the preaching of the prophets, especially Second Isaiah who portrayed the return from Babylon as a new exodus (Isa. 43:2; 51:9–11). Likewise, the important Sinai tradition is constantly reinterpreted in the Old Testament—probably originally and orally as a place of theophany (Exod. 19:16–19), then as a combination of theophany and covenant (Exod. 24:9–11), finally as a covenant tradition with no concern for theophany (Exod. 24:3–8; the Book of Deuteronomy). Thus, the mere mention of, or allusion to, a certain tradition in a biblical text does not enable the interpreter to conclude automatically that he has before him "the same old story." That "old story" may be so reinterpreted by the author, speaker, or editor of the passage that the tradition says something new to his generation.

5. The *context* of the passage deserves particular attention by the interpreter, because at whatever level separate pieces were brought together—as sources, by editors, by redactors—some sequence or arrangement gave structure to the compiler's work. When dealing with any portion of chapters 7 and 8 of the Book of Isaiah, it is important to observe that the former chapter is biographical and the latter, autobiographical. However, the two chapters stand together because they deal with the same historical period, the Syro-Ephraimite crisis. This context may indeed make a difference when examining any portion of the section.

Likewise in the Ten Commandments at Exod. 20:1–17, the interpreter must recognize the obvious fact that the act of salvation (Exodus 14) precedes the giving of the law. Thus the laws of the Decalogue are given not in order for the people to be saved but rather because they already have been saved. These laws are, then, guides for the way redeemed Israel ought to live. Now whether or not the present Christian interpreter accepts the "Third use of the law" (the commandments as guidelines for the way redeemed *Christians* should live), nevertheless the context shows that God's imperative follows rather than precedes God's indicative. That this sequence is also a New Testament pattern, one need only compare the structure of Paul's letter to the Romans.

Thus, the relationship of a passage to nearby verses, paragraphs, and chapters, as well as the position of a unit in the outline of a book or collection of books (such as the Tetrateuch), sheds much light on its intended use and meaning at various levels in its history.

e. Construct an interpretative rendering of the passage. Now that individual tasks of exegeting the text have been accomplished, it is time to pull together some of the results of this work. One helpful method of getting it together is to paraphrase the passage by employing everything which has been learned in the preceding steps. For example, the "working text" at Isa. 7:10 might have read "Again the Lord spoke to Ahaz, ..." On the basis of the study of *literary matters* (the importance of the adverb "again"), *context* (the preceding speech in 7:1–9 and verse 13 which indicates that the Lord is again speaking through Isaiah), and the *historical situation* (the Syro-Ephraimite crisis of 735–34 B.C. with its threat of deposing the Davidic king), the interpreter might paraphrase the verse as "In the midst of the Syro-Ephraimite threat against the Davidic throne in 735 B.C., the Lord spoke to Ahaz, the Davidic King of Judah, through his spokesman Isaiah, in much the same way that he did in verses 1–9 where he promised that the threat would not come to pass."

Now what did the text mean? Finally, the exegete must summarize what meaning the text had at its various levels (oral stage, sources, redactions, contexts). In order to be consistent with an understanding of the Bible which gives witness to a God who speaks and acts, then the question "What is God doing here?" must be asked of each level. Such a question should be answered in a single sentence which describes the situation or the problem as a theological dilemma to which God, as subject of the sentence, addresses his word of comfort and of challenge. The interpreter might now have before him two, three, or four such theological statements which were, in fact, different proclamations to God's people in various circumstances of life.

2. WHAT THE TEXT MEANS

Not all proclamations or interpretations of a text are valid or suitable for Christian proclamation at a given time. It has been asserted that a Christian approaches the Old Testament with faith commitments and presuppositions, and, in a sense, reads the Old Testament through the New. It has also been said that such a stance might render unacceptable certain blocks of testimony. Thus, the Christian must go so far as to determine which levels of an event are appropriate or inappropriate from Christian proclamation, which interpretations are legitimate or illegitimate for proclaiming the God who is known to us as the Father of Jesus Christ.

Now the unpopular "canon within the canon" principle is applied not only to books and pericopes but to the levels of tradition and interpretations of each pericope. To return to some of the possibilities already cited, there is no difficulty in proclaiming the Word of God from Exodus 14 on the basis of the Yahwist's "The Lord redeems his people who stand still in faith." Also quite proclaimable is the Word on the basis of the total passage: "God redeems his people from a bondage from which they are unable and even unwilling to save themselves." But one would have to exercise caution with the Priest's proclamation "In the midst of the conflicts of his people God comes to prove he is Lord by showing his strength and by getting glory over his enemies." The God whom we know as the Father of Jesus Christ indeed judges men because of their sin, but he does not slaughter those who persecute his people in order for the church to shout "My god can lick your god!"

Now when there are several levels of interpretation which might be vehicles for proclaiming the Word of God, how does the Christian proclaimer decide on which to use? The answer to that can only be made on the basis of the situation of the audience which is to be addressed. Since the expression of the Word of God is always dependent on the situation which is being addressed, then the interpreter has another task: to exegete the contemporary scene, the audience, the problem. For it is only in knowing the present situation that the proclaimer can select the level of the text which should be employed as the vehicle for the Word; it is only in making the Word relevant to that situation that the message becomes proclamation!

Thus, what is valid or legitimate in the proclamation of the Yahwist, the Priest, Isaiah, or Ezekiel is dependent upon the theological stance of the Christian interpreter. What is appropriate in choosing which of the several legitimate theologies to use as the sermon text is determined by the situation in which the proclaimer finds his audience.

An obvious difficulty presents itself at this point: How does the interpreter move from the level of proclamation he has chosen (his selected "text sentence") to his own sermon? By carefully analyzing the situation of the text and the situation he must address, the preacher may find it necessary to sharpen the text's problem, to narrow it or to broaden it, so that, without doing injustice to theological problems of the text, he can more directly speak to his own situation. For example, suppose the preacher chooses as his text sentence the proclamation of the final editor of Exod. 14:10–31: "God redeems his people from a bondage from which they are unable and even unwilling to save themselves." The bondage is the problem: in the text it is the physical enslavement of one people to another and their apparent destruction; the theological problem at stake is the apparent threat to God's promise of freedom in the Promised Land. To the Christian preacher that bondage from which men are unable and even unwilling to save themselves is the power of sin. Whether or not the preacher decides to change the wording of his text sentence in order to begin composition of a sermon sentence, nevertheless the movement from the one "bondage" to the other deserves careful consideration in the outline of the sermon. Likewise, the theological answer or response to the problem needs some careful attention, since the rescue of the people by God in the text is not identical to the Christian's understanding of redemption or salvation which is accomplished on the cross. Thus, moving from the selected text sentence to the sermon sentence, the preacher might now be prepared to summarize his sermon and use as his outline the sentence "From that constraining and overwhelming force which entices us to wallow in our own destructive pessimism, God sets us free by giving his Son to die on the cross." A simple outline for such a sermon might be something like the following:

I. Problem: An Overwhelming Force Entices Us to Wallow in Pessimism
   A. Today's pessimism as a result of a broken trust in God's promises
      1. The realities of modern life in which evil and violence seem to prevail
      2. The credibility gap involved in comparing these realities to the church's proclamation that the age of salvation is here
   B. Israel's pessimism in Exod. 14:10–31 as a result of apparent discrepancies in God's promises through Moses
      1. The reality of the onrushing Egyptian army
      2. The distrust in the proclamation of Moses that freedom and a new life awaited them

II. Response: God Sets Us Free
   A. Israel's God conquered the enemy as well as his people's wills to fulfill his promise of freedom in the Promised Land
      1. Moses' call to trust God in the face of overpowering odds
      2. God accomplished the deliverance he had promised
   B. In his Son's death on the cross God once and for all set us free to be at home in his presence
      1. The church's call to hear what God *has done* in Christ
      2. God's accomplishment of reconciliation with himself and the ultimate consummation of that relationship

This outline has the advantage of starting and ending with the present situation and of keeping the biblical story intact for the sake of continuity. Many other possibilities are available, of course, but such an outline as the above works easily and naturally out of the type of text and sermon sentences which have been described. The content and structure hopefully are consistent with the entire approach described in this work.

PART TWO

PROCLAMATIONS OF

SELECTED TEXTS

Numbers

21:4–9

1. ESTABLISHING A WORKING TEXT
A literal rendering of the Hebrew text

And they journeyed from Mount Hor in the direction of the Reed Sea to go around the land of Edom, and the breath of the people became short on the journey. And the people spoke against Elohim and against Moses, "Have you brought us up from Egypt to die in the wilderness? For there is no food and no water, and our throat has felt a sickening dread at the contemptible food." And Yahweh sent forth against the people the *saraph* serpents, and they bit the people, and a multitude of the people died. And the people came to Moses and said, "We have sinned, for we spoke against Yahweh and against you. Pray to Yahweh that he might turn the serpent(s) from us." And Moses did pray on behalf of the people. And Yahweh said to Moses, "Make for yourself a *saraph* and place it upon a standard, so that anyone who is bitten might look at it and live." And Moses made a bronze serpent and placed it on the standard; and if the serpent(s) bit a man, he would look at the bronze serpent and live.

A comparison of some English translations

In setting side by side the *Revised Standard Version*, the *New English Bible*, and *The Torah: The Five Books of Moses*[1] one quickly notices that the only substantial differences occur in connec-

1. *The Torah: The Five Books of Moses* (Philadelphia: The Jewish Publication Society of America, 1962).

tion with the name of the serpents (verses 6 and 8) and with the expression in verses 8 and 9 which variously render "set it on a pole" (*RSV*), "mount it on a standard" (*The Torah*), or "erect it as a standard" (*NEB*). These slight differences present no major difficulty in accepting any one of the three translations as a working text. The major difference between the translations cited and the literal translation from the Hebrew occurs at verse 4 where "the breath of the people became short on the journey" is obviously an idiom which needs some attention under literary matters.

2. SETTING IN LIFE

The possibility of a serpent attack on the ancestors of Israel is very real, and so the historicity of the event cannot be dismissed outright. However, in light of the fact that nomads often encountered serpents in the wilderness, the emphasis on the situation in this passage seems to fall on the cultural or sociological rather than the historical background. The nomads' fear of the wilderness as the abode of deadly serpents is attested both here and at Isa. 30:6.

But the situation here is difficult to determine precisely, because there are several mythological and folkloristic elements intertwined in this story. One can see in the serpent image to which Moses made an allusion the serpent as a symbol of healing in the ancient world. And more generally, making a serpent image as a cure for snake bite reflects the magical notion, also common in the ancient world, that a plague or a demon can be warded off by making a replica of it (cf. 1 Sam. 6:1–5).

3. LITERARY MATTERS

The author of the original story is impossible to identify, if indeed one can speak of an author at all. The story seems to be similar to so many Tetrateuchal stories in which we are dealing more with a whole series of storytellers rather than with a literary author. At the same time, it is impossible to date the original version of the story, although, as will be indicated later, it seems to have originated in a nomadic situation.

A study of the problems connected with the terminology bears little fruit. As is evident from the work on establishing the text, the words for the serpent(s) are problematic. The Hebrew word *srp* may or may not be related to the verb *saraph* meaning "to burn," and so *srp* serpents may or may not be "fiery" or "venomous." The problem is further complicated by the fact that the word *srp* is used both as a qualifying word for "serpent" (*nāḥās*) in verse 8 and as a substitute for that noun in verse 6. Unfortunately, no amount of work in lexicons or concordances will lead to a satisfactory conclusion.

Especially interesting, however, in verse 4 is the idiom "the breath of the people became short on the journey." The use of the Hebrew verb *hiqṣîr* ("became short") with words for "breath" has a special meaning. When used with *nepeš* (as here) and with *rûaḥ*, both of which mean "breath" or "wind," *hiqṣîr* points to "reaching one's limit of endurance" (cf. Job 21:4, Judg. 16:16, Mic. 2:7, Zech. 11:8, Judg. 10:16). The last two of these references show that the object of utter discouragement is introduced, as in our verse 4, by the preposition *b* which can mean "in, on, by, with near, at," etc. The meaning of the idiom at Num. 21:4, then, seems to be "the people reached their limit of endurance with the journey." In other words, it is not simply that "*on* the way" they became discouraged at something or someone. Rather they became discouraged with the journey itself.

4. THE CRITICISMS

Form-critically it must be stated at the outset that the piece is a narrative. Furthermore, on the basis of what was said concerning the setting in life, the story seems to reach back to an oral period of transmission when Israel's ancestors lived in a nomadic or seminomadic state. Having moved from that early stage to a later development, the story might have become an etiology, i.e., a story used to explain the origin of a name or place or cultic practice. What the story might explain is the origin of the symbol called "Nehushtan" which was a bronze serpent in the Jerusalem temple (see 2 Kings 18:4). In other words, the story at Num. 21:4 might have been used in order to give some authenticity to the Canaanite object which stood in Jerusalem's temple. The author of 2 Kings 18:4 makes precisely that connection, but the relationship is not so clearly indicated in our story. Thus, the classification of the account as an etiological narrative can only remain a possibility.

A quick glance at the story could also lead to its classification as a fairy tale, particularly because, as the narrative stands, there seems to be an emphasis on the magical aspect of the bronze serpent. While such a tendency is present in the story there are other emphases as well. The notion of the people complaining against God and Moses points to a common motif in the wilderness narratives in Exodus and Numbers, namely, the so-called murmuring motif.

Finally, the interpreter must consider the whole story in its present context and conclude that in some way it has become a historical saga; i.e., it deals with the migrations of tribes through the wilderness ("historical"), and it speaks of a direct intervention of God in the affairs of men ("saga").

Now, however, we must move on to discuss *source* analysis. In spite of the different words used for the serpent, the passage seems to be a unity rather than an intermingling of sources. There are not discernible two narratives which can be set side by side; neither is there evident one basic narrative with loosely attached fragments from another. The only piece of evidence which appears to lead to source differentiation is the use of the divine names Elohim and Yahweh: Elohim (God) appears at verse 5, but elsewhere in the story the name Yahweh (the Lord) is repeated. This terminology could account for a distinction between the Yahwistic and Elohistic or Priestly sources. But without evidence of two strands of material, the name change can better be explained as the work of the JE redactor who, it can be shown elsewhere, used both names in order to give cohesiveness to his account. Furthermore, the Elohist himself could have used the name Yahweh in this story, because, according to E, the name Yahweh had already been revealed to Moses (Exod. 3:14–15). Because of this possibility and because the murmuring motif elsewhere seems usually to be E,[2] we conclude that the narrative comes from the pen of the Elohist.

Thus it seems that the Elohist took over an old fairy tale about the magical snake-bite cure and edited it in such a way as to establish a motive for the serpent attack (the murmuring motif) and to

---

2. This generally held assumption has been recently challenged, however, by George W. Coats, *Rebellion in the Wilderness* (Nashville: Abingdon Press, 1968).

proclaim that God was the one who provided (or at least initiated) the means for the deliverance. The Elohist's proclamation seems to be: *When his people scorn and reject God's act of deliverance and his way to fulfillment, God judges their rebellion but nevertheless acts to save the rebels.* Or by emphasizing the common murmuring motif in the wilderness stories, the proclamation of E might be stated: *God directs his people in spite of themselves and even against their wills toward the accomplishment and fulfillment of his promise.*

The *tradition* of this event is reinterpreted at Deut. 8:15 where it is part of a sermon (verses 11–20) which proclaims the gracious acts of Yahweh from the exodus through the wilderness to the giving of the Promised Land. In this reinterpretation there is no use of the murmuring motif, no complaining by the people. Rather, the use of the tradition in Deuteronomy 8 is to stress that God brought his people through difficult situations in order "that he might humble you and test you, to do you good in the end." This wisdom-like proclamation of the story is: *God, far from granting his redeemed people immunity from danger, brings them and preserves them through such trouble in order to refine them in the knowledge that whatever they have and are is due to God's gracious faithfulness.*

In the New Testament the story of Num. 21:4–9 is cited by Paul at 1 Cor. 10:9–10 as an example or instruction for Christians who put the Lord to the test. The event is also used somewhat allegorically (probably, more accurately, typologically) by the author of the Gospel according to St. John, where Jesus proclaims: *Just as the uplifted serpent served as God's means of drawing men to himself to preserve their lives, so the crucified Son of man is God's act of drawing men to himself for the gift of eternal life* (John 3:14–15).

5. CONTEXT

The context of a passage can be as narrow as the preceding and following paragraphs or as broad as the Bible itself. Perhaps the most significant context for this passage is the recognition that it belongs to the wilderness traditions which are between the salvation event of Exodus 14 and the Sinai traditions of Exodus 19–24 on the one side and the settlement of the land on the other. In other words, the event takes place *after* the act of deliverance but *before* the fulfillment of the promise of land for which the people were delivered. At Exodus 3, in the revelation to Moses, God promises to deliver his people from Egypt in order to take them to the Promised Land. In our passage the redemption from slavery has occurred, but the final outcome of that promise is yet to be realized. Thus, the people are "on the way," and it is this journey, the time of waiting, the frustration of not yet experiencing the land, which irritates the people and causes them to murmur against God and his spokesman Moses.

6. Interpretative Rendering

The only refinements or interpretative renderings to be made in this passage on the basis of our investigation occur at the beginning and at the end. Verse 4 can be paraphrased ". . . and the people, already delivered but not yet at the Promised Land, reached the limit of their endurance with the journey. And so, they murmured against God. . . ." Verse 9 might be made clearer by the rendering "And so Moses made a bronze serpent and set it on a standard, and if the serpent(s) bit a man, the man would look at the raised bronze serpent by which God drew the man to himself in order to preserve his life."

7. Theologies of the Passage

When the proclamations of the event are set down, then the various possibilities seem to be as follows:

a. Some nomads, attacked by serpents, managed to survive by making a symbol of a serpent which healed those who looked at it (the original oral stage: a fairy tale).

b. When his people scorn and reject God's act of deliverance and his way to fulfillment, God judges their rebellion but acts to save the rebels (the Elohist's redaction).

c. God directs his people in spite of themselves and even against their wills toward the accomplishment and fulfillment of his promise (the murmuring motif; again probably E).

d. God brings his people and preserves them through trouble in order to refine them in the knowledge that whatever they have and are is due to God's gracious faithfulness (Deut. 8:15–16).

e. God confronts his people on the frustrating road between redemption and fulfillment—judging them when they reject his deliverance and preserving them when they look to him in faith (the E account with particular emphasis on the present context of the passage).

When these theologies come into contact with that of the Christian interpreter, the first possibility can be promptly eliminated. The other proclamations will be refined (or corrected) in the sense that the redemption of God with which we are involved is the decisive act in Christ, and the fulfillment to which we look forward is the consummation of God's kingdom which has already been ushered in by that Christ event. But we too are *on the way*; we too become discouraged with waiting, with the journey; we too, though delivered, rebel against God in our frustration; and so also God comes to meet us on the way, judging us and rescuing us in the midst of our rebellion.

Whether the Christian preacher chooses to base his sermon on Num. 21:4-9 by using the second, third, or fifth interpretations depends on the situation in which he finds his audience. If the fourth interpretation is more appropriate to that situation, then he should use as his text Deut. 8:11-20 and speak that message.

Genesis

22:1–19

1. Establishing the Working Text

Because of the length of this text and because the literal translation from the Hebrew offers nothing substantially different, such a translation is not presented here. Moreover, even a comparison of several English translations presents no major difficulties in accepting any one of them as a working text. However, while virtually all English translations read "the land of Moriah" at verse 2, such unanimity is not present in ancient translations of the phrase. Ancient renderings range from "the land of the Amorites" (Syriac) to "the land of the vision" (Vulgate and others) or to "the lofty land" (Septuagint). Some of these renderings are possible by slightly emending the Hebrew text. However, one of the basic principles in establishing the original text (textual criticism) is to accept the most difficult reading as the most probable original one. In this case, "the land of Moriah" is certainly the most difficult reading, because no one knows where such a land is located. Therefore, "the land of Moriah" is the generally accepted reading.

Of greatest importance in this text is to determine the scope of the text. The pericope listed in the lectionaries includes verses 1–14, but it is obvious that the story continues as far as verse 19. Whether or not the interpreter decides to limit himself to the first fourteen verses can only be determined *after* the exegetical work is done. For the purpose of establishing a working text, then, the scope of the passage is Gen. 22:1–19.

Once the text includes verses 15–19, however, an interesting comparison is evident in verse 18: the *RSV* translates ". . . shall all the nations of the earth bless themselves"; the *AV* reads ". . . shall all the nations of the earth be blessed . . ."; and the *NEB*, "All nations on earth shall pray to be blessed as your descendants are blessed. . . ." The difficulty here is due to the Hebrew verb form which most literally means "bless themselves" (*RSV*). But what does such an expression mean?

2. LITERARY MATTERS

The two problems raised above deserve attention first. "The land of Moriah" (verse 2) is not attested as such elsewhere in the Old Testament. But "Mount Moriah" occurs at 2 Chron. 3:1 as a substitute for Mount Zion where Solomon built the temple. This only other occurrence can lead to two possible conclusions: (a) There really was a land of Moriah connected to the Abraham story which became unknown to later generations in Israel. Because the important Abraham-Isaac incident was said to have occurred at this place, the writer of Chronicles used the title as a substitute for Zion in order to make the reader think that the temple was built on the same hill where that old revelation took place. (b) The writer of Chronicles was the first to use the name Moriah (for what reason is impossible to say), and because that name was a substitute for Zion in the Chronicler's work, a still later editor inserted it in Genesis 22. In either case, a relationship between the hill on which the Abraham event took place and the mount on which Solomon built his temple seems to be intentional by someone. By whom or when this probable relationship took place is now impossible to determine, but the relationship certainly added an important tradition to the site on which the temple stood.

As for the problem in translating the blessing formula, the Hebrew verb here is clearly a reflexive one (*hithpaʿel*), and that same verb form is used in the same formula at Gen. 26:4. Elsewhere, however, at Gen. 12:3; 18:18; 28:14, the blessing formula employs a different form of the verb (*niphʿal*) which can be either passive or reflexive, i.e., "be blessed" or "bless themselves." Thus the weight of the evidence seems to fall on the reflexive since all occurrences of the blessing formula in the patriarchal stories would be consistent with that use. When it comes to determining the meaning of such an expression, a concordance will reveal that the word *bless* appears in the strictly reflexive (*hithpaēl*) form at Deut. 29:19; Isa. 65:16; Jer. 4:2; and Ps. 72:17. In Deuteronomy 29 and in Jeremiah 4, the term seems to mean "to boast," the latter in the positive sense of boasting in Yahweh, the former in the negative sense of boasting in a false sense of security. At Ps. 72:17 men "bless themselves" in Jerusalem's king. And so, it seems that the reflexive use of the word means "consider oneself fortunate" on the basis of something or someone. In this respect, Gen. 22:18 might best be rendered "and because of your descendants shall all the nations of the earth consider themselves fortunate." This expression would mean that the fame of Israel-to-be will be seen and in some sense shared by all men.

In addition to these two problems, several others deserve mention. At verse 8 the Hebrew verb *r'h* "to see" is used in the sense of "provide." The only other case in which this common verb seems to have the same meaning is at Deut. 33:21 where "see" makes little sense: "He *furnished* for himself the best of the land"; thus, at least one parallel can be cited as evidence for the use of *r'h* as "provide" in Gen. 22:8. However, in verse 14, where the same word occurs twice in connection with the meaning of the place name, it is not clear whether the translation should be "So Abraham called the name of the place Yahweh-yireh; as it is said until this day, 'On the mount of the Lord it will be provided' "; or "So Abraham . . . , 'On the mount of the Lord he appears (is to be seen).' " We shall return to this problem in our study of form criticism.

Several times in the narrative God addresses Abraham by name (announced once in verse 1 and twice in verse 11), to which Abraham responds (as he does also to his son in verse 7), "Here I am." This address by God of a person's name (usually repeated twice), followed by this response, occurs also at Exod. 3:4; 1 Sam. 3:4–10; and, without mention of the person's name, the response appears at Isa. 6:8. The repeated use of this expression seems to indicate a formula of some kind used when God singles out individuals for some task.

3. THE SETTING IN LIFE

The situation in the ancient world which immediately comes to mind in reading the narrative is the practice of child sacrifice. The Old Testament testifies to the atrocious practice at 2 Kings 16:3; Jer. 7:31; 19:5; 32:35; Ezek. 16:20–24; 20:31, as a custom which some Israelites borrowed from their Canaanite neighbors. In addition, laws against such a practice are expressly stated at Deut. 12:29–31; 18:9–12, with permission granted to use an animal as a substitute for a child at Exod. 13:11–16. There also exists evidence from Mesopotamia and from Canaan which seems to affirm that these biblical passages are not unfounded.[1]

4. THE CRITICISMS

Source analysis deserves attention first. There exists abundant evidence that the story before us is almost exclusively E. The common characteristics of E which are present here include (a) the use of the word God (Elohim) at verses 1, 3, 8, 9, and 12; (b) the notion that God tests men (verse 1) appears in the E passage at Exod. 20:20; (c) the purpose of such testing is to determine if one fears God (verse 12); again compare Exod. 20:20; (d) God is so transcendent for E (he speaks "from heaven") that he always uses mediators to confront and address man; here, as often, it is an angel (verses 11, 15); (e) the description of the multitude of descendants at verse 17 is quite similar to the descriptions of E elsewhere (cf. Gen. 15:5).

At the same time, there are some non-Elohistic elements in the story: the use of the name Yahweh (the Lord) at verses 11, 14, 15, and 16; and the blessing formula for all nations at verse 18. Both these characteristics are typical of J. In addition, the Elohist's concern was for northern (Israelite) sanctuaries, but the "mount of the Lord" in verse 14 seems to be an allusion to Jerusalem's Mount Zion.

If one removes the characteristic elements of E from the narrative in order to work back to an original *oral form*, then it seems that we have before us a story which served as a polemic against

---

1. See Theodor H. Gaster, "Sacrifices and Offerings, OT," in *The Interpreter's Dictionary of the Bible*, vol 4 (Nashville: Abingdon Press, 1962), 153–154.

child sacrifice—much like the legal prescriptions from Deuteronomy and Exodus mentioned above. The original form would then have had a polemical intention, and its proclamation would have been: *Undesirous of the sacrifice of children, God himself provided an animal as a substitute.*

One could also argue that the narrative should be classified as an etiological saga, insofar as it might have been told to explain the origin of the name of the place *Yahweh-yireh.* Recent studies have demonstrated, however, that very few Old Testament narratives were composed for this purpose; even the formula "as it is said until this day," which appears at verse 14, seems to have been added to an already existing story.

Thus, it is our conclusion that the story was originally a polemic against child sacrifice. When Elohist took up the old story and edited it according to his interests, the story became something quite different. From his introduction in verse 1 to the announcement that Abraham was a God-fearer (verse 12) and on to the reward for his piety (verses 16–17), the Elohist has made the story into a wisdom tale in which God tested Abraham in order to learn where his heart was and to reward him because it was in the right place. In wisdom literature such testing and discipline refines men and brings them closer to God. In this sense the proclamation of the Elohist might be summarized: *When God makes unreasonable demands on men, he is testing their faith in order to refine them and reward their obedience.*

Now the presence of the name *Yahweh* (the Lord) in several places in the narrative and the use of the blessing formula at verse 18 does not seem to be sufficient evidence to argue that a J version of the story is intertwined with E. The story seems rather to be a unity; it cannot be divided into two separate strands. Thus, the use of the name and the blessing formula are probably the result of the *redactor* who supplied some J characteristics in order to provide continuity within his JE story.

This mention of continuity should lead directly to the question of context, but first let us consider how the *tradition* was used in the Bible. It is astonishing to note that, in spite of its popularity today, the incident, or better, the tradition, is mentioned nowhere else in the Old Testament. In the New Testament the story is used in several places as E intended: as an example of the way the man of faith acts (Heb. 6:13–14; 11:12, 17–19; James 2:12). But the New Testament writers are interested also in the promise of God (verses 16–18) and not simply in Abraham's faith (cf. Luke 1:73; Acts 3:25; Gal. 3:16 where Paul allegorically relates Isaac and Christ). But this same promise used in these New Testament passages appears in other Genesis stories, and so one cannot be certain that they refer specifically to Genesis 22.

5. CONTEXT

The continuity of the JE document and the continuing reference in the Genesis narratives to God's promise of descendants and blessing makes the context of Gen. 22:1–19 particularly important. The redactor JE wove his material together in such a way as to provide continuity, and at the same time he set the structure of the narratives which the final redactor followed.

Now in the structure of the Genesis narratives, the one thread which continues from Genesis 12 to the Joseph story is the promise of God concerning land and descendants (J adds the blessing formula). This promise is repeated by God in spite of the patriarchs' weaknesses and in spite of all other obstacles. From Genesis 12 to chapter 21 Abraham waited for God to start working out his promise of descendants. Finally, when Abraham was more than a hundred years old, God gave him a son, the first of many descendants to come. One chapter after the birth of Isaac is recorded God asks Abraham to sacrifice this only child and, thereby, jeopardize the fulfillment to what had been promised so long. This story, in other words, presents a contradiction of God to Abraham, but he nevertheless responds obediently, and God continues the way of his promise.

The inclusion of verses 15–19 emphasizes this continuing promise which began in Gen. 12:1–3. These verses, furthermore, point toward the future, as the promise of God constantly does.

6. INTERPRETATIVE RENDERING

In light of the previous work some paraphrases at certain points in the passage might help to pull together isolated bits of important information. The context might enable the interpreter to render verse 1 as "After these things God seemed to contradict himself by testing Abraham with the command that he sacrifice his only son Isaac, on whom the promise of descendants depended." Furthermore, one could add here, "While God seemed to be asking what the gods of the Canaanites and others asked regularly, he addressed Abraham in a way that seems to have singled out the patriarch for a special task." (This interpretation combines both the setting in life and the literary matter concerning the meaning of God's address to a man, followed by "Here I am.") In verses 11 and 15 the significance of the use of the angel and the phrase "from heaven" might be paraphrased as "the transcendent God spoke through his mediator." And in light of the word study on "bless themselves," the promise at verse 18 might be stated as "and because of your descendants shall all the nations of the earth consider themselves fortunate at seeing and sharing in the fame of Israel."

7. THEOLOGIES OF THE PASSAGE

Work on the text has indicated at least three levels of proclamation in the narrative. First, there was the proclamation of the oral stage which proclaimed that God accepted and desired the sacrifice of animals rather than children. Second, there was the theology of the Elohist who used the piece like a wisdom storyteller in order to show that God's testing refines men and ultimately leads to reward for obedience (fear of God). Now, third, when the entire story is seen in its context of the way of promise and when the custom of the problem of child sacrifice is combined with that promise, then the theology of the whole passage seems to be: *Through his apparent contradictions God brings men to commit themselves in faith, refining the relationship between them and setting them apart from the world in which they live.*

The first of these proclamations is legitimate, to be sure. However, in our society where child sacrifice is not practiced, it is irrelevant. It must be stated, though, that this interpretation might be the most useful one for a foreign missionary working in the midst of a tribe which still sacrifices children. Such a possibility must remain open. The proclamation of the Elohist sounds too much like the theology of old optimistic wisdom by which the righteous are rewarded, and the wicked are punished. There might be some other way to interpret E's theology in this text which would make it more legitimate for the proclamation of the gospel. The third interpretation of the whole passage with emphasis on the present context seems to provide the basis for a sermon which proclaims the described action of God through the means of his Son's death on the cross. This death of the Christ/Messiah, in fact, is the Bible's great contradiction, but through this scandal God brings men into a relationship with himself and thereby sets them apart in the world to be his instruments of blessing.

Genesis

32:22–32

1. Establishing a Working Text

A comparison of the English translations in the *RSV*, the *NEB*, and *The Torah* reveals only a few differences between the third mentioned and the first two. At verse 28, *RSV* and *NEB* are similar in translating ". . . for you have striven (strove) with God and with men, and have prevailed." *The Torah* at this point—which, like the Hebrew text, is verse 29—reads the same in a footnote but in the text the expression is translated ". . . for you have striven with beings divine and human and have prevailed." Likewise at verse 30 where *RSV* and *NEB* read "I have seen God face to face . . .," *The Torah* translates, "I have seen a divine being face to face. . . ." In both cases the offensive thought of Jacob wrestling with God is softened by the translators of *The Torah* by their rendition of *Elohim* as "divine being."

The only other noteworthy difference in the three translations considered appears at verse 29. *RSV*'s ". . . And there he blessed him" is quite similar to *NEB*'s ". . . but he gave him his blessing there." But *The Torah* translates, "And he took leave of him there."

A literal translation from the Hebrew is not presented here because the translation of the *RSV* in this passage is quite literal and can serve as a working text.

2. Literary Matters

The passage belongs to the collection of stories known as the Jacob cycle. Like most other such stories in the Tetrateuch, the

84

question of the identity and date of the author is not relevant.
Most of these stories come from an oral tradition and cannot be
assigned to an author who composed them.

The story itself is strikingly untheological in its terminology,
and so the search for key words on which to carry out word studies
ends in vain. Likewise, there are no obvious idioms here to investi-
gate.

The "man" who came to wrestle with Jacob (verses 24, 25)
remains quite anonymous and unidentifiable until verse 30 when
Jacob announces that it was God. Apparently this realization came
to him when the "man" said, "You have striven with God . . ." in
the previous verse. When this identification of the "man" with
"God" is made, it is tempting to do a word study on "wrestle" in
order to discover other cases of God wrestling with men. Unfortunately, the word (Hebrew *'abaq*) occurs only in this passage.

Perhaps the greatest literary problem in the passage lies in the
explanation of the name Israel. The one offered here, namely, "you
have striven with God and with men and have prevailed" is impossible. But then almost every such explanation in the Old Testament
is wrong from a scientific or etymological standpoint. If the name
Israel is at all related to the Hebrew word *sārāh* "to persist" or "to
persevere" (and that is indeed debatable), then the explanation
would have to be translated as "God perseveres," or "May God
persevere." The explanation "you have striven with God," like
almost all such explanations, is based on a word play due to simi-
larity in sound rather than an accuracy in grammar.

3. SETTING IN LIFE

The tone of the whole story sounds quite unhistorical, and so
the setting is probably to be understood culturally or sociologically
rather than as an incident which actually occurred. In the midst of
such elements in the story as blessing, dietary taboo, and place
names, there stands out above all else the change of Jacob's name
to Israel. This change may be significant in two ways.

First, it is clear from reading the Old Testament that, while
Jacob is usually the name of the patriarch, it is used also, especially
in poetic literature, as the name for the nation. Likewise, while
Israel is usually the name of the nation, that name is sometimes

employed to speak of the patriarch. With that flexibility of terminology in mind, the interpreter cannot always be certain that a
given text is speaking of the individual or the nation. A narrative
or a poetic reference to Jacob, might, in fact, be an allusion to or a
description of the experience of the nation. But why should the
narrative go to such pains to relate the two names? Or, more basic,
why are there two names for the patriarch and two for the nation
(*cf. infra* pp. 127)? An answer to such a question involves a complicated set of presuppositions and a lack of solid evidence. It
seems, however, that in the days before Israel became a twelve tribe
league a group of tribes named Israel and another group under the
name Jacob merged to form a larger unit which further incorporated
a few other tribes in order to establish a twelve tribe system. To provide unity in this merger, the traditions of the separate groups
became intermingled to form one pre-history, and, further,
"Israel" became identified with "Jacob." This identification is
explained here in the dramatic story about Jacob wrestling with
God; the equation is made much less dramatically by the Priestly
writer at Gen. 35:10 where the name "change" is simply
announced by God in Paddan-aram.

Second, the emphasis on "name" in the story must be understood also in light of the ancient Semitic understanding of a person's name. For us a name is simply a matter of *identification*; it is
something we have by which others can recognize us and address
us. For the ancient Semites, however, the name was far more
important; for them it was a matter of *identity*. A man did *not*
simply *have* his name; he *was* his name. The person and his name
were so inseparably bound up together that to know one's name
was to know him in his very being. This knowledge of a name
meant that one could influence and exercise control over the other,
precisely because the knowledge and use of the name were so inti-
mately related to the knowledge and use of the person himself. In
this way we can understand that when man named the animals in
Gen. 2:19–20, he was given the same dominion and control as
that accorded to him in the Priestly account of creation at Gen.
1:28.

This understanding of the name helps to interpret our story in
two respects. (a) The change of Jacob's name to Israel could indi-

cate that the man himself was thereby changed. If person and name are virtually identical, then the change of one should imply the change of the other. The meaning of Jacob's name had been variously explained, as can be seen in the earlier chapters about this patriarch. When he was born, we are told that he came out of the womb hanging on to his brother's heel (*'āqēb*; therefore, he was named *Ya'aqob* (Gen. 25:24-26). When the twins had grown up, however, and when Esau found himself the victim of his brother's conniving ways, Esau exclaimed that his twin was rightly named *Ya'aqob* "because he has cheated (*'āqab*) me twice" (Gen. 27:36). Now if this second explanation was remembered by the narrator of our story about Jacob at the Jabbok, then the intention of the name change might have been to announce that Jacob would now be different. Now with his name as "may God persevere," the patriarch is quite different from his prior life when he was called "he cheats."

(b) The request by Jacob to learn the name of his opponent (verse 29) came after it had been revealed to him that he had spent the night wrestling with God (verse 28). The request by a man to learn the name of a god or divine being is an obvious attempt to gain control of the deity, to use him for one's own purposes, in effect, to acquire a genie. In the Old Testament such a request appears also at Judg. 13:17 when, Manoah, though not yet convinced that the herald of the birth of a son is a divine being, asked the visitor for his name. The response of "the angel of the Lord" (verse 22 indicates it was God) is the same as that of the Jacob story: "Why do you ask my name . . . ?" In neither case does God give his name. The only other request for God's name is made most subtly by Moses when God commands him to return from Midian to lead the people out of Egypt (Exod. 3:13). In this case God does provide a name, according to the Elohist, but the name "I am who I am" is such that God maintains his freedom while nevertheless giving a name to be used in the cult. Thus, in these three attempts by man to get control of God by seeking his name, God remains in complete control. In Genesis 32, Jacob ends up without a name but with a blessing, and the wrestling God vanishes before the sun appears on the horizon.

4. THE CRITICISMS

Apart from the contradiction of verses 22 and 23 concerning whether or not Jacob crossed the river Jabbok, there seems to be little evidence to indicate a conflation of several sources. To be sure, the story does not run smoothly, and indeed there are many diverse elements in the story. But the unevenness and the diversity cannot be explained by a division into sources. The piece seems to be a unity.

Most scholars argue that the story belongs to the Yahwistic *source*.[1] This identification is based, not primarily on terminology, but on the nature of the activity and by a process of elimination. Neither the Elohist with his insistence on God's transcendence nor the Priest with his lofty view of God and his glory could be responsible for writing a story in which God wrestles with a man and barely comes out the winner. The Yahwist, however, displays a fondness of such stories, as when he half-humorously reports the argument between Yahweh and Abraham concerning the fate of Sodom (Gen. 18:22–33). Furthermore, the unity of the people expressed by the identification of Jacob and Israel is an important emphasis in the days of David and Solomon when the Yahwist seems to have been active.

How much of the story belongs to the Yahwist, and how much was added by later editors is difficult to determine. *Form-critically,* as the passage stands before us, it is clearly a narrative and, beyond that, it is a saga in which God intervenes into the affairs of men. Moreover, at the end of the story, it becomes clear that the saga is an etiological one—threefold! There are explained the origins of the name Israel, the name Peniel, and a cultic dietary taboo. Whether or not the Yahwist is responsible for any or for all of these etiologies is questionable. It must be stated that the last two of these (verses 30–32) seem to be attached to the narrative rather arbitrarily and do not seem to be significantly related to the story which precedes. Just why "Peniel" is included here is difficult to say, although the explanation about seeing God's face makes clear to the reader of the final story the identity of the nocturnal wres-

---

1. For a summary of views concerning the passage and for an excellent study of the whole story, see Gene M. Tucker, *Form Criticism of the Old Testament* (Philadelphia: Fortress Press, 1971), pp. 41–54.

tler. The etiology concerning the dietary law at verse 32 is even more difficult to comprehend, because such a law is attested nowhere else in the Old Testament. At some time in Israel's history the taboo meant something to someone, but more than that profound statement cannot be said.

Let us assume, on the basis of the loose connection of verses 30–32, that the last two etiologies were added to the Yahwist's story: the one about Peniel to emphasize the identity of the "man"; the dietary practice for some unknown reason. Such an assumption would mean that the Yahwist's account ends at verse 29, at which Jacob, refused by his adversary to reveal his name, nevertheless ends up with a blessing. Because of the identification of "Israel" and "Jacob," two originally separate groups which made up the nation before and during the Davidic-Solomonic Empire, it is possible that the Yahwist is responsible for the etiology of "Israel." The important part of verse 28 for the Yahwist, however, is the name change itself and not the meaning of "Israel" (cf. the announcement of the same name change by the Priest at 35:10 where no explanation of the meaning of Israel appears).

Now if the exegete reads verses 22–26, he is left without any indication of a source. But more important, without the Yahwist's verses 27–29, the story tells of a nocturnal encounter between a hero (Jacob) and some sort of superhuman character who uses a magical touch to finally overcome his opponent. This character seems to be recognized by Jacob as a divine being from whom the patriarch asks a blessing. He must return to his abode before daylight, and he appears to wrestle before the hero crosses the river (verse 24 seems to indicate Jacob had not yet crossed the Jabbok). Thus, it seems that the original form was a hero saga in which someone special to a storyteller overcame a nocturnal river demon before crossing the demon's river. While a precise parallel story cannot be cited, there are numerous parallels from the ancient world for river gods and for nocturnal demons.[2]

Somewhere along the oral pipeline, the story became attached to Jacob who apparently was one of those individuals around whom such stories accumulated. The Yahwist, by a few significant *redac-*

---

2. See Theodor H. Gaster, *Myth, Legend, and Custom in the Old Testament* (New York: Harper & Row, 1969), pp. 205–210.

tional additions in verses 27–29, demythologized the story into an encounter between God and Jacob, the end result of which is the change of (or identification of) Jacob to Israel. This result comes about not by Jacob controlling God but by God remaining in complete control and freedom. In light of his theological and nationalistic interests the proclamation of the Yahwist seems to be: *As a result of a personal encounter, God brings his people into existence and blesses them.* (Unfortunately, the content of the blessing is not stated explicitly in this passage as it is in 35:9–11.)

The etiological additions to this apparent Yahwistic piece in verses 30–32 add nothing of theological value. The explanation concerning the "face of God" obviously had meaning for the people at the (cultic?) place Peniel, but they have little meaning for us apart from the emphasis that the wrestler was really God. The dietary practice which follows has nothing to say to us today.

The *tradition* of God's encounter with Jacob at the Jabbok appears elsewhere in the Old Testament at Hos. 12:3–4 where it is part of a Jacob cycle in which events in his life are used negatively. In order to establish the nation's guilt, Hosea points in a pejorative sense to the career of their ancestor whose shady dealings began while he was still in the womb and continued into his manhood when he brazenly strove with God. The details of Hosea's account show that he uses the episode recorded in Genesis 32 loosely and, in fact, in a way no longer evident in the Genesis story. However, his use of the word *strove* (*śārāh*) in verses 3 and 4 demonstrates that the term was related to the Jabbok incident as early as the eighth century B.C., and so the explanation of "Israel" as the one who "strove with God and with man and prevailed" must pre-date Hosea and probably goes back at least to the time of the Yahwist. Why a northerner (Hosea) uses the Jacob tradition negatively and why a southerner (Yahwist) employs it positively is now impossible to answer.

At any rate, Hosea goes on in verses 4–6 to proclaim that just as Israel's proud and brazen ancestor was brought to tears and supplication, so the Israel of the eighth century must repent and entreat the favor of God in order to avoid utter disaster.[3]

---

3. See the fine commentary on this passage by James Luther Mays, *Hosea*, "The Old Testament Library" (Philadelphia: Westminster Press, 1969), pp. 161–165.

5. CONTEXT

It is generally agreed and somewhat obvious that the story of Jacob at the Jabbok stands out like a sore thumb in the movement of the surrounding material. The transition from verse 21 (or maybe 22) to the incident is not at all smooth, and the further movement from verse 32 into the following chapter is worse. The unit under consideration, in other words, seems to have been an independent piece which was inserted into the present context. Without its presence one could move easily and smoothly from 32:21 to 33:1. What then might have been the purpose of the redactor who inserted this intrusion into the total narrative? In the first place, it is interesting to note in the context of the Jacob cycle that when the patriarch left his home and fled from his brother Esau (Gen. 27:41-45), God encountered Jacob at Bethel and promised him, among other things, a safe return (Gen. 28:10-20). Jacob's stay in Haran with his uncle Laban is, for the most part, recorded without reference to God-appearances (although God remains active in his life; cf. 31:10-13). Now when Jacob is returning home to meet Esau after all this time, the compiler tells us that God again confronts Jacob. In other words, the JE redactor has put the material together in such a way that the episode of Jacob with Laban and away from Esau is surrounded by encounters with God. Thus the intrusion of our story into the present context can be explained as due to the outline of the redactor.

Second, placed as it now is, immediately before the long-feared meeting with Esau, the encounter with God at the Jabbok seems to prepare the way for Jacob to face this crisis. When the interpreter recalls the significance of the name in the story, that a name change implies a change in the person himself, then he can look for the results of that change in the following episode. When Jacob meets his brother whom he cheated and from whom he fled years earlier, the patriarch approaches Esau as a new man—humble, generous, grateful, affectionate. Thus, in its present context the story announces: *In the midst of the crises of life God wrestles with men to change them, to make them face the problem as different persons.*

6. INTERPRETATIVE RENDERING

On the basis of the various stages of the process, the resulting rendition of the story should include some reference to the "man" in verses 24–25 and to the significance of the name change. Thus, one might render verse 24*b* as "and God, in the form of a man, wrestled with him. . . ." Likewise, verse 25 might read: "When the deity in the guise of a man. . . ." Verses 28–29 seem to mean: "Then he said, 'Your name shall no longer be Jacob ("the cheater") but Israel, "the one who has striven with God and men and has persisted." Thus, you yourself will now be different as well.' Then Jacob asked God for his name, in order to use him for his own purposes, but in typical fashion, the God of the Old Testament refused to give up his name and his freedom. He departed from Jacob leaving him an unidentifiable blessing."

7. THEOLOGIES OF THE PASSAGE

The passage presents one of the most bizarre portrayals of God in the whole Bible, and yet in spite of the mythical and folkloristic backgrounds, in spite of etiologies which have little meaning for today, the passage can speak to Christians in several ways.

The proclamation of the Yahwist that *as a result of a personal encounter God brings his people into existence and blesses them* is a testimony which the Christian can use to speak of God's creation of the church, his election of the new people of God, through his encounter with us in and through his risen Son. One can become a "new man" only when God comes to wrestle down the "old man."

When the passage is seen in its context, the proclamation of the JE redactor is slightly different: *In the midst of the crises of life God wrestles with men to change them, to make them face the problem as different persons.* In the day to day crises which beset his people, God comes to be present, and he comes in his Word whenever one Christian proclaims it to another. His coming, if it means anything at all, has an effect on men—sometimes accusing, sometimes comforting, but nevertheless an effect which makes a difference in the man's life. The difference in the man which occurs again and again makes a difference in the way he handles fears, anxieties, troubles of all sorts. Life cannot be the same when the Word—that God sent his Son to die for our sakes—is addressed to men in their crises.

Isaiah

35:1–10

A literal rendering of the Hebrew text

1. ESTABLISHING A WORKING TEXT

1 (The) wilderness and (the) dry land shall exult,
    and (the) desert shall rejoice and sprout;
like a fresh shoot of a reed ²it shall sprout vigorously,
    yea it shall rejoice (with) joy and a ringing cry.
The glory of Lebanon shall be given to it,
    the splendor of Carmel and Sharon.
They shall behold the glory of Yahweh,
    the splendor of our God.
3 Make strong (the) weak hands,
    and make firm (the) tottering knees.
4 Say to those who are rapid of heart,
    "Be strong! Do not fear!
Behold your God, (with) vengeance he will come,
    (with) the recompense of God he will come in order to set you free."
5 Then the eyes of (the) blind shall be opened,
    and the ears of (the) deaf shall be opened.
6 Then (the) lame (one) shall leap again and again like a stag,
    and the tongue of (the) dumb shall ring out;
for in the wilderness waters will burst open,
    and rivers in the desert.

93

7 And the parched ground shall become a pool,
    and (the) thirsty ground, springs of water.
In the habitation of jackals (shall be) her resting
place,
    (their) haunt (shall become) reeds and rushes.
8 And there shall be a highway and a road,
    and it shall be called "The way of holiness."
(The) unclean shall not pass over it,
    and he (shall be) for them a traveler of the road,
    and fools shall not wander erroneously (on it).
9 There shall not be there a lion,
    and a violent beast shall not ascend it;
    it shall not be found there.
10 But those who are redeemed shall travel,
    and those who are the ransomed of Yahweh shall
return.
And they shall enter Zion with a ringing cry,
    and the joy of eternity (shall be) upon their
head(s).
Exultation and joy they shall attain,
    and sorrow and groaning shall flee away.

A Comparison of Some English Translations

Setting side by side various English translations of the passage
shows that the differences are primarily stylistic rather than substantive. A few verses, however, stand out with differences which
demonstrate some confusion with the Hebrew text itself.

Verses 1–2: The *RSV* and *AV* state the mood of verbs in a firm
and positive indicative (as in my translation above), while the
NEB renders according to the jussive in Hebrew: "Let the wilderness . . . be glad," etc.

Verse 1: The type of flora at the end of the verse is rendered "as
the rose" (*AV*), "like the crocus" (*RSV*), and "with fields of
asphodel" (*NEB*). Moreover, the position of the phrase is different in these translations.

Verse 7: The second half of the verse, precisely because it is difficult to understand in Hebrew, is translated differently in the three
sources used here; the *RSV* considers the animals "jackals," *NEB*

renders "wolves," and *AV* "dragons." But the translation of the whole line is the major problem.

Verse 8: The most difficult portion of the whole passage occurs near the end of the verse. *NEB* translates "it shall become a pilgrim's way" (adding a footnote to the effect that the Hebrew is unintelligible); *AV* reads "but it shall be for those: the wayfaring men. . . ." *RSV* omits the problem entirely by assigning "it and he is for them a wayfarer" to a footnote.

2. LITERARY MATTERS

It would be fruitless to attempt to solve all the problems with the text, precisely because the Hebrew text is extremely difficult, if not corrupt at several points. However, for the sake of methodology, note that the translations cited do not offer in the last half of verse 7 a synonymous parallelism, which is expected both of the poetic structure and the entire lists of contrasts in verses 1–2, 5–7. My own translation attempts to maintain this structure of poetry, but nevertheless "(shall be) her resting place" still presents problems.

More important in this passage is the determination of authorship. Although the passage appears in the first thirty-nine chapters of the Book of Isaiah, the style, terminology, and content indicate that the author is not the prophet of the eighth century but Second Isaiah of the exilic period. Some of the reasons for this judgment are as follows: the use of the word *'ap* "then" in verses 5 and 6 is typical of Second Isaiah (cf. 40:24; 41:20, 26; 42:13; 43:7, 19; 46:11); the Hebrew expression behind "springs of water" in verse 7 occurs elsewhere in the Old Testament only at Isa. 49:10; the announcement in verse 4 is quite similar to that of Isa. 40:10 (and virtually identical to Isa. 62:11, the author of which seems to be a student of the exilic prophet); the highway of verse 8 sounds like that of Isa. 40:3; 43:19–20; and the notion that Yahweh changes the wilderness into a place of glory can be seen elsewhere at Isa. 41:18–19. In fact, virtually every verse in the chapter bears striking similarities with the anonymous prophet of the exile. Such an assignment of authorship dates the passage at the end of the exile (just before 540 B.C.) and sets the place and audience in Babylon.

Some key words appear here which deserve attention, for the

interpreter must attempt to determine what "wilderness," "venge-ance," "redeemed," "ransomed," and "save" meant for Second Isaiah and his audience. The exegete might begin by using a Bible dictionary at this point; particularly interesting points, or insuffi-cient information, might then lead to the use of a concordance.

"Wilderness" in the Old Testament generally is a place of anxi-ety and loneliness where man might at any time be attacked by vicious beasts and snakes; cf. Num. 21:4–9; Deut. 8:15. But most important is the use of the word in the same author. Even a quick glance at a concordance reveals that the wilderness is a place of loneliness and desolation (Isa. 50:2) but that Yahweh comes to change it into a place of joy (Isa. 41:18–19; 51:3) and by build-ing a highway in the wilderness (Isa. 40:3; 43:19–20).

This "highway" (verse 8) in Second Isaiah may be a deliberate attempt by the prophet to employ a piece of Babylonian religion in a polemical way. At every New Year festival in Babylon (the Akitu), the Babylonian deity Marduk was carried in procession, escorted by the king, down a stone paving called the Sacred Way. The prophet uses this imagery of "the way of holiness" to announce that Israel's God Yahweh will come to take them home.

"Vengeance" (verse 4) is used by Second Isaiah (and Third Isaiah as well) to point to something positive for Irsael (61:2; 63:4) but negative for Israel's enemies (47:3; 59:17). The "redeemed" (Hebrew $g'l$) of verse 9 are those who have been released in a court case (i.e., set free from forced servitude) by the intervention of a kinsman known as the redeemer ($g\bar{o}'\bar{e}l$). This concept of Yahweh as redeemer of his people occurs thirteen times in the work of Second Isaiah; the fact that it appears only five times elsewhere in the Old Testament is indicative of the impor-tance of the term in addressing exiles. Standing in synonymous parallelism with "redeemed" are "the ransomed of Yahweh." That God pays a ransom to free his people is attested at Deut. 7:8; 13:6; Mic. 6:4, etc., in reference to the exodus from Egypt; from exile God ransoms his people at Jer. 31:11; Zech. 10:8; and, most important, Isa. 51:11 which is exactly identical in expression to 35:10. As for the term *save* in verse 4, a Bible dictionary or a Hebrew to English lexicon will explain that salvation in the Old Testament really means "to give spaciousness to (someone)," thus freedom from constraint and confinement. Second Isaiah proclaims that no idol, no diviner, no one, in fact, can save the people (45:20; 46:7; 47:13, 15); only Yahweh can save, and he has promised to do so (43:12; 49:25; cf. also 59:1).

Of particular interest in the study of terminology is the expression in verse 6 *waters will burst open*. This precise combination of Hebrew words occurs at Exod. 14:21 to describe the act of God in dividing the Reed Sea to allow the Hebrews to pass through. The use of this phrase is not accidental. That the return from exile in Babylon is conceived by Second Isaiah as a new exodus can be seen elsewhere at 40:3, 10, 11; especially 43:14–21; 48:10, 20–22; 50:2; 51:9–11.[1]

Finally, throughout the whole chapter is a consistent use of synonymous parallelism. The interpreter must bear this feature of poetry in mind for the purpose of understanding each line in light of the preceding or following line.

3. THE SETTING IN LIFE

A reading of the passage indicates that the situation to which the text is addressed is one of fear and trembling, a state of despair and hopelessness. The text proclaims a coming day of joy, and to describe that coming event it contrasts with what is apparently the situation: one which is portrayed in terms of a bleak desert, of despair, of blindness, deafness, dumbness. All these are terms of confinement, all the opposite of *shalom*. Moreover, the situation is one from which the people need to be redeemed in order to return to Zion from which they are apparently separated.

Such a situation could be seen in the time of the prophet Isaiah, for in 721 B.C. the Assyrian army had devastated the northern kingdom Israel and had carried off the leaders of the people to exile (who knows where?). Therefore, Isaiah *could* be addressing those exiles with the message that Yahweh would come to bring them to Mount Zion with all these signs. However, on the basis of literary matters we have already discussed, most scholars agree that the text is the work of Second Isaiah. He is addressing those

---

1. For a discussion on Second Isaiah and the exodus, see Walter E. Rast's *Tradition History and the Old Testament* (Philadelphia: Fortress Press, 1972), pp. 63–68.

people of Jerusalem who have been exiled in Babylon for fifty years and who long to "return" to Zion (in this situation "return" to Zion makes more sense than if the prophet Isaiah were preaching to northerners). Thus it seems that the historical situation is the time near the end of the Babylonian exile (ca. 540 B.C.) when the people had grown tired of hoping for deliverance, when God seemed to have either called off the covenant arrangement or was destroyed along with the Temple in 586, when plainly the exiles were in a hopeless state in face of the overwhelming powers which constrained them. The more we can learn of the people's attitudes in this period, the more relevant and concrete the message of the text becomes. To that situation the prophet announces that God comes to save, to turn the whole situation around, to turn hopelessness into joy, death into life. Therefore, fear not.

4. THE CRITICISMS

Since we are dealing here not with material from the Tetrateuch, source criticism plays no part in exegeting the passage. The first concern then is related to *form*. Verses 3–4 can be classified as an "announcement of salvation."[2] This form is directed to a situation of distress and announces, by the use of the future verb (Hebrew imperfect), something which is about to happen. It is an announcement of the end of the distress by a coming event of God. Verses 1–2, 5–10 provide the structure and content of the form called "portrayal of salvation" which contrasts the external nature of the present condition to the external nature of the new situation to come. This definition of forms does not add anything of a substantive nature to what we have already said about the passage. However, in this case the meaning of the passage is made sharper by showing that this *contrast* between distress and salvation, present condition and future condition, is not accidental to the proclamation of the passage but integral to it. This contrast, essential to the theology of the text, must be taken seriously by the present-day proclaimer.

Under the study of *tradition* criticism we need to mention again

2. For a description of "salvation" forms, see Claus Westermann, "The Way of the Promise through the Old Testament" in *The Old Testament and Christian Faith*, ed. Bernhard W. Anderson (New York: Harper & Row, 1963), pp. 200–224, esp. pp. 202–209.

that Second Isaiah interpreted the release from Babylonian exile as
a new exodus. In this respect the old tradition concerning the
bursting open of waters (Exod. 14:21) is repeated at verse 6.
Moreover, the whole description of the triumphal march through
the wilderness to Jerusalem is quite reminiscent of the delivery of
Israel's ancestors from Egypt. The prophet of the exile is emphatic
about his concern that the old tradition of the exodus be remembered, but at the same time he speaks loudly and clearly that the
hope of the people is not based on that past event but on a *new* act
of God, a *new* exodus, which will even surpass the old exodus in
splendor (see especially Isa. 43:18–19). The old tradition has
become an announcement of a future act of salvation. In chapter 35
the prophet accomplishes this purpose by combining an announcement of salvation with a portrayal of salvation, as he did elsewhere
in his preaching.

5. CONTEXT

The context of Isaiah 35, if the judgment is correct that the
author is Second Isaiah, is not important for understanding the
original piece. Who knows where it stood originally, or what was
the context in which it stood? It should probably be interpreted as
a sermon in its own right, i.e., with no surrounding material necessary to understand it. At the same time, it must be stated that
someone—a later redactor—saw some reason to insert the sermon
at this point. In its present position it follows an announcement of
judgment against Edom; in the description of the results of God's
judgment there appears some terminology which is similar to some
expressions in chapter 35. For example, "the haunt of jackals"
(34:13; 35:7). In all probability, however, the final compiler who
combined Isaiah 1–39 with 40–66 uses the sermon of chapter 35
as a transition from the one prophet to the other. In spite of a continuing number of chapters (36–39), chapter 35 is the last sermon
attributed by the final redactor to the prophet Isaiah. This context
leads then directly to chapter 40.

6. INTERPRETATIVE RENDERING

On the basis of the prior investigation, one might paraphrase
verses 1–2: "God-forsakenness and desolation shall be turned into

the joy of his glorious presence." Verses 3–4: "Spread the news to the anxious and fearful, 'God is coming! He will bring comfort for you and disaster for those who oppress you. He will come with his benefits to give you freedom from your confinement.' " Verses 5–7 seem to mean: "All the unpleasantness you have suffered will become ecstasy; even nature will be changed when he comes." Verses 8–10 seem to mean: "You all know about that Sacred Way on which Marduk travels every New Year's day! Well, watch closely! Yahweh, our God, is coming down that Way to lead us home in joy."

7. THEOLOGY OF THE PASSAGE

The passage seems to be a unity—one sermon—which proclaims: *From the confinement of despair, hopelessness, God-forsakenness, the Lord comes to rescue his people to the joy of freedom in his presence.* That God comes in Christ, through the proclaimed Word, to bring to himself a hopeless and despaired people is a message which needs to be heard in our day.

Micah

3:9–12

1. ESTABLISHING A WORKING TEXT

A literal translation from the Hebrew·

9 Hear this, O heads of the house of Jacob,
    O rulers of the house of Israel,
  who regard justice as an abomination,
    and make crooked all that is straight,
10 who build Zion with bloodshed,
    and Jerusalem with violent unjust deeds.
11 Its heads make judgments on the basis of a bribe,
    and its priests teach for the sake of a reward,
    and its prophets practice divination for money.
  But they lean upon Yahweh, saying,
    "Is not Yahweh in our midst?
    Harm cannot come upon us."
12 Therefore, on account of you,
    Zion will be plowed like a field,
      and Jerusalem will become a heap of ruins,
      and the mount of the house, thicket-covered heights.

A comparison of English translations

For the most part, the differences which occur among English translations is due to the use of synonyms rather than to any substantive disagreement. It should be noted, however, that the literal rendering at verse 11 "they lean upon . . ." is retained by *RSV* but is interpreted as "men rely upon . . ." in *NEB*. Furthermore, in the last line of the passage, the literal "and the mount of the house, thicket-covered heights" is basically the same as *RSV*'s "and the mountain of the house a wooded height," but *NEB* interprets the line as "and the temple hill rough heath."

2. LITERARY MATTERS

Because of the style and content of the passage, virtually every Old Testament commentator regards this piece as the preaching of the prophet Micah. In fact, even the most ruthless of scholars consider chapters 1–3 of the book to be original with Micah (with the possible exception of 2:12–13). Thus, there is little debate that the author is the prophet Micah and that the passage dates from the lifetime of that eighth-century prophet. But some literary expressions in the passage deserve some attention.

Verse 9: "house of Jacob" and "house of Israel." While these designations usually refer to the northern kingdom, they are used here (and at 2:7 and 3:1) to point specifically to the southern kingdom of Judah. This identification is clear from the references to Zion and Jerusalem in verse 12.

Verse 11: "on the basis of a bribe." A word study of the Hebrew *šōḥad* or "bribe" reveals that the word is used for a gift offered in order to pervert justice; cf. Isa. 1:23; 5:23; 33:15; Prov. 17:8; 21:14, etc.

Verse 11: "for the sake of a reward." The use of a concordance shows that the Hebrew *m^{e}ḥîr* (*AV* and *RSV* translate "hire") can have both positive and negative connotations. However, standing in synonymous parallelism with *šōḥad* "bribe," as it does also at Isa. 45:13, the meaning here must be negative.

Verse 11: "lean upon Yahweh." Again the use of a concordance will immediately make clear the meaning of the expression. "Lean upon Yahweh" (*šā^{e}n 'al YHWH*) means to "trust in him, to rely upon him" (cf. Isa. 10:20; 2 Chron. 13:18; 14:11; 16:7, 8). Likewise, "lean upon God" (*šā^{e}n 'al '^{e}lohîm*) has the same meaning at Isa. 50:10. It stands to reason that "leaning upon" someone or something other than the Lord is interpreted as rebellion; cf. Isa. 31:1; Ezek. 29:7. Thus, *NEB*'s rendering "rely upon" is quite appropriate.

Verse 12: "the house." The use of the definite article points to a definite or particular house, maybe the "well-known" house. In parallelism with Zion and Jerusalem, "*the* house" can only mean "the temple" and should be translated accordingly (so *NEB*).

Verse 12: "thicket-covered heights." A word study of Hebrew *ya'ar* (to use *Young's Concordance*, follow *AV*'s translation as "forest") demonstrates that *ya'ar* can be "forest" in a good or neutral sense. More often, however, the word has a negative meaning: a hiding place for fugitives (1 Sam. 22:5), a place of feared wild beasts (Amos 3:4; Mic. 5:7; Jer. 5:6), and as a place of desolation (Isa. 21:13). In the light of these results, the parallelism with the two preceding lines is quite consistent.

3. SETTING IN LIFE

One could spend much time describing the period in which Micah lived, i.e., the second half of the eighth century B.C. There could be much said about the invading kings of Assyria who made Judah a tax-paying member of that empire in return for saving her from the Syro-Ephraimite alliance in 734 B.C., who brought the northern kingdom Israel to her knees and to obliteration in 721 B.C., who besieged Jerusalem when Hezekiah tried to assert independence in 701. It may be that fear or threat from Assyria prompted Micah to speak of the destruction of Jerusalem which had hitherto been regarded as indestructible.

It seems that from rather early days in the monarchy of Israel, there persisted a tradition about the inviolability of Jerusalem and her temple. Apparently because God had chosen Jerusalem as his appointed site to dwell with his people, the Jerusalemites developed this tradition that the city and its temple could never fall. Such an idea is reflected in some ancient psalms (see especially Psalm 48) and, surprisingly, in the preaching of Isaiah.[1] Micah, who was Isaiah's contemporary, had other ideas about the fate of the city and the temple which led to Judah's false optimism.

Equally important for this passage is an understanding of the internal corruption in the leadership of Judah and the oppression of the weak by the strong. Martin Noth[2] argues that the large

---

1. For a discussion of the use of this tradition in the preaching of Isaiah, see Gerhard von Rad, *Old Testament Theology*, vol. 2, trans. D. M. G. Stalker (New York: Harper & Row, 1965), pp. 155–169.

2. Martin Noth, *The History of Israel*, 2d rev. ed. (New York: Harper & Row, 1960), pp. 216 ff.

political structure of the monarchy begun with David demanded an urban foundation, so that efficient administration and specialization of life in industry and commerce could take place. Under this urbanization a money economy developed and consequentially a separation between the rich and the poor. Thus, from the eighth-century prophets—Amos, Hosea, Isaiah, and Micah—came denunciations against the upper and ruling classes. These prophets preached disaster from Yahweh because of the injustices in society and because of reliance on false, external forms of worship. None of them denounced worship or the cult *per se.* Rather what they fumed against in the name of God was the emphasis on the external forms over against true worship in the life of the community. It is against this background of increasing social injustice and in the light of eighth-century prophecy that the passage must be interpreted.

4. The Criticisms

The most important criticism with which the preacher has to deal in such a prophetic sermon is *form.* The content of the text indicates that the passage is a speech of judgment. Moreover, since the speech is addressed not to an individual but to Israel, it can be called an *announcement of judgment against Israel.*[3] Some scholars refer to it as a combination of diatribe and threat. In either case, what is important in naming or classifying the form is to determine the characteristics of that form, other passages with which this one might be compared, and then to ask the redactional question concerning the particular use of the form by our author.

The characteristics of the announcement of judgment can best be seen in the following outline:

$$
\begin{array}{l}
\text{Reason} \left\{
\begin{array}{l}
\text{Introduction} \\
\text{Accusation} \\
\text{Development}
\end{array}
\right. \\
\quad\text{Messenger formula: "Therefore ..."} \\
\text{Announcement} \left\{
\begin{array}{l}
\text{Intervention of God} \\
\text{Results of intervention}
\end{array}
\right.
\end{array}
$$

3. For a description and analysis of various judgment speeches in the preachings of the prophets, see the work by Claus Westermann, *Basic Forms of Prophetic Speech,* trans. H. C. White (Philadelphia: Westminster Press, 1967).

This same basic outline can be seen in such prophetic sermons as Amos 4:1–2; Hos. 2:5–7; Isa. 8:6–8; 30:8–14; Mic. 3:1–2, 4; 2:1–4; Jer. 5:10–14; 7:16–18, 20. In our own passage the *introduction* begins in verse 9 with the call to hear and continues to the word *Israel*; the *accusation* occurs in the rest of verse 9; and the *development* of the accusation occupies verses 10 and 11. The *messenger formula*, "Therefore, on account of you," appears at the beginning of verse 12; and the *announcement* of judgment itself is the total concern of the remainder of verse 12. Now in this announcement the intervention of God is not explicit; Yahweh or Elohim is not mentioned. But according to the pattern of the announcement of judgment, it seems safe to assume that the disaster of verse 12 will not be the result of an accident but the result of the direct intervention of God. By the use of this formula, Micah makes a proclamation of what God is about to do even though the preacher uses rather passive descriptions to portray what will happen.

As to *tradition criticism* in this passage, there are two features worthy of note. First is the rejection in this sermon of the old tradition about the indestructibility of Zion. Micah has not simply reinterpreted that ancient concept; he has proclaimed that there is no truth in it. Second, the passage itself became a tradition of a sort. More than one hundred years after it was spoken, the judgment announcement was quoted by the elders of Jerusalem in order to save Jeremiah's life when that prophet was about to be executed for prophesying the destruction of Jerusalem. Precedent showed that Hezekiah did not execute Micah. Why then should Jeremiah be put to death for the same prophecy (see Jer. 26:16–19)?

5. CONTEXT

In this case the literary context is not so crucial as it is in some of the other passages we have considered. It is important to see this sermon in the midst of other—equally separate—sermons in the first three chapters of Micah. In the context of his preaching as a whole, we can better interpret any particular sermon. Equally important, however, is the context of the eighth-century prophets and their preaching of judgment against the nation which has been discussed above.

6. INTERPRETATIVE RENDERING

Now hear this, leaders of Judah:
> you are accused for hating justice and twisting uprightness,
> for building up Jerusalem and Zion with bloodshed and violence.

Your evil has resulted in and is illustrated by
> your leaders making judgments for bribes,
> your priests giving spiritual instruction for graft,
> your prophets making prophecies for money.

And yet they piously and optimistically rely on the Lord:
> "Is not the Lord among us, for we have the temple?
> Surely, then, no disaster can befall us."

Now here comes the message: Because you do all this,
> Zion, your holy hill, shall be plowed level as a field;
> Jerusalem, your city of invincibility, shall become ruins;
> and the temple hill, where you consider me to be present,
> > will become a high thicket where only jackals, robbers,
> > and fear will be found.

7. THEOLOGY OF THE PASSAGE

The proclamation of Micah to his nation seems to be this: *When the leaders of his people condone and further the injustices of the rich against the poor and rely on the false security of God's favor and presence, the Lord destroys the symbols of their false security.* Or to put it more simply and ironically, *When false optimism concerning God's presence corrupts the faith which acts in love and justice, God makes himself absent from his people.*

To proclaim such a message from a Christian pulpit is, of course, to preach a sermon which is law, i.e., the Word accusing men. While some might argue that the gospel needs to be set alongside this accusation in the same sermon, such a position is neither consistent with the biblical testimony to God (in either Testament), nor true to a dynamic understanding of God's Word by which he confronts men in their pride and apathy. In one's total ministry in a parish or other situation, a preacher need not lay out his entire systematic theology in each and every sermon, and so there is room to preach now and again a sermon which proclaims God's Word as law.

To return to the theology of the passage and the situation Micah was addressing, it is quite possible that the situation to be addressed today is one in which the audience's optimism is misplaced, that no harm can come to a church or a nation which has many external signs of prestige and power. Neither is it impossible to imagine a situation in which, because of these external signs of prestige, a church or a society ignores and thus condones injustice and oppression. In such situations it is precisely the law which must be proclaimed, and to interpret the result of such audacity as separation from God is entirely consistent with the revelation of God as it is witnessed in the New Testament. The proclamation of Micah that God would make himself absent from his people by destroying the very symbol of his presence among them is indeed one which drives men to the need of a Savior.

Isaiah

7:10–17

1. Establishing a Working Text
A literal translation of the Hebrew

¹⁰And Yahweh again spoke to Ahaz saying, ¹¹"Ask for yourself a sign from Yahweh, your God: Make it as deep as Sheol or as high as the heavens." ¹²And Ahaz said, "I will not ask and I will not put the Lord to the test!" ¹³And he said, "Listen, O house of David: Is it too little that you exhaust the patience of men, that you exhaust my God's patience also? ¹⁴Therefore, the Lord will give you a sign: Behold, the young woman is pregnant and she will bear a son, and she will call his name 'Immanu-'el. ¹⁵Curds and honey he will eat, when he knows to refuse what is harmful and to choose what is good. ¹⁶For before the lad knows to refuse what is harmful and to choose what is good, the land before whose two kings you are afraid will be forsaken. ¹⁷And Yahweh will bring upon you and upon your people and upon the house of your father days which have not come since the day of the turning aside of Ephraim from Judah—the king of Assyria."

A comparison of English translations

Differences in the first four and a half verses among various English translations are merely stylistic. The problems begin, however, in the second half of verse 14 where the content of the sign is described.

> Verse 14*b*: *AV*: "Behold, a virgin shall conceive and bear a
> son, . . ."

> RSV: "Behold, a young woman shall conceive and
>   bear a son, . . ."
> NEB: "A young woman is with child, and she will
>   bear a son, . . ."
> Kaiser: "if a young woman, who is now pregnant,
>   bear a son, . . ."[1]

The differences here are significant. The *AV* alone regards the woman as a "virgin," while the others speak of her as being a certain age but without reference to her sexual experience (or lack of it). Both *AV* and *RSV* view the conception as taking place in the future; *NEB* and Kaiser agree on the chronology, but differ on the understanding of the woman. *NEB* seems to have in mind a particular pregnant woman, but Kaiser intends a general or collective situation in which any pregnant women might bear male children.

> Verse 15:   AV: "Butter and honey shall he eat, that he may
>   know to refuse the evil, and choose the good."
>   RSV: "He shall eat curds and honey when he knows
>   how to refuse the evil and choose the good."
>   NEB: "By the time that he has learnt to reject evil
>   and choose good, he will be eating curds and
>   honey; . . ."
>   Kaiser: "Cream and honey shall he eat, when he knows
>   how to refuse evil and choose good."

Only the *AV* considers the food as that which will enable the young man to refuse evil and choose good. The other translations simply indicate that at a certain age (when he can distinguish good and evil), his diet will consist of curds and honey. In this latter respect, the literal rendering above is in agreement with *RSV, NEB*, and Kaiser. My own translation differs from all of these in one respect, however; where they read "evil," I translate "harmful" because the Hebrew word *ra'* does not necessarily have moral overtones.

In verse 16 the *AV* alone translates in such a way that the feared land will be forsaken of her kings; the other translations, including my literal rendering, understand that the land, before whose kings Judah trembles, will be deserted. At the end of verse 17, all

---

1. See Otto Kaiser's commentary on *Isaiah 1–12*, trans. R. A. Wilson, "The Old Testament Library" (Philadelphia: Westminster Press, 1972) p. 96.

the translations, except *NEB*, retain the problematical "the king of Assyria" which appears in the Hebrew text.

2. SETTING IN LIFE

Because of the nature of the material in this and the surrounding passages, it is helpful to discuss the *Sitz im Leben* before analyzing the literary aspects of the piece. The passage 7:1–9:6 of the Book of Isaiah is almost universally agreed to be Isaianic in origin and to date from the period of the Syro-Ephraimite crisis which occurred about 735–34 B.C.

The Assyrian Empire, under its powerful king Tiglath-Pileser III, was spreading westward with the intention of gaining complete control of Palestine, an important crossroad at the east end of the Mediterranean. Ruling over the northern kingdom Israel at this time was a certain Pekah, who along with the king of Damascus, Rezin, decided to form a coalition to stop Tiglath-Pileser's move. Naturally, the two northern kings wanted the king of Judah—first Jotham and then his son Ahaz—to join the resistance. Out of fear of the Assyrians' power, Ahaz refused his northern neighbors. Therefore, Pekah and Rezin decided to move first against Judah, depose Ahaz, and put their own crony—an Aramean known only as the son of Tabeel (Isa. 7:6)—on the throne, so that Judah would become part of the alliance. Against Isaiah's advice that Ahaz trust in the Lord, Judah's king deemed it wiser to put his confidence and his tribute in the hands of Tiglath-Pileser, who would prevent the Syro-Ephraimite coalition from deposing him. Ahaz's plan did, in fact, work, but as a result he became eternally "grateful" for the Assyrian's help.

To understand Isaiah's plea to Ahaz that he do nothing in the face of this crisis, the interpreter must remember that Ahaz was a member of the Davidic dynasty which had been promised by Yahweh himself that one of David's descendants would forever remain on Jerusalem's throne (see 2 Samuel 7). With this promise from the Lord as a background, it was utter rebellion on Ahaz's part to trust the power of a political alliance rather than the faithfulness of Yahweh.[2]

2. For further reading on the Syro-Ephraimite crisis, see Martin Noth, *The History of Israel*, 2nd rev. ed. (New York: Harper & Row, 1960), pp. 257 ff.; or John Bright, *A History of Israel* (Philadelphia: Westminster Press, 1959), pp. 256–257.

3. LITERARY MATTERS

Verse 10: The adverb *again* (expressed in Hebrew by a verb) is significant here because it obviously ties the speech of our text to a previous speech—apparently concerning the same issue. That previous speech in verses 1–9 of the same chapter reports that Yahweh, through his messenger Isaiah, promises Ahaz that the alliance formed to depose him will not be successful.

Verse 11: Isaiah's reference to "your God" indicates a relationship between Yahweh and Ahaz which might indicate simply that Ahaz is a member of the covenant community or might point specifically to the special relationship between Yahweh and the king on Jerusalem's throne (cf. Ps. 2:7). In any case, the use of the pronoun shows that Isaiah is announcing that the authority of his message is based upon a word from the God with whom Ahaz has a special relationship. This word is neither from Isaiah himself nor from a strange deity but from "*your* God."

Verse 12: A word study of "test" or "tempt" (Hebrew *nisseh*) shows that Ahaz was acting in a somewhat commendable way, because elsewhere in the Old Testament "testing the Lord" is considered a grave offense; see Pss. 95:9; 78:18, 41, 56; 106:14; Exod. 17:2, 7; Num. 14:22; Deut. 6:16. But one gets the impression in our text that the king is mouthing pious hypocrisy. His refusal to ask for a sign, while pious from one point of view, can also be understood as his refusal to change his plans of seeking help from Assyria. Ahaz had his own—probably popular—plan to escape disaster. Since he already knew from the previous speech (verses 1–9) that Yahweh's plan was different, he did not want a sign or a message or anything else from Yahweh.

Verse 13: Isaiah's response "Listen, O house of David" calls attention to the dynasty of which Ahaz was a member and simultaneously highlights the problem: the threat to the Davidic dynasty. Moreover, the summons to hear, followed by a vocative, is reminiscent of the announcement of judgment we studied at Micah 3:9–12. Furthermore, the question which Isaiah puts to the king sounds like the "accusing question" which is common in judgment announcements (cf. Jer. 2:4–13, especially verse 5; Mic. 6:1–8). This question contains an interesting switch from Isaiah's previous sentence: in verse 11 he spoke to Ahaz about "your God"; now, after Ahaz's hypocritical response, Isaiah speaks of "my God."

Verse 14: "the young woman." The article is used in Hebrew to designate something or someone known to everyone, or something or someone to whom the speaker can point. For example, when Obadiah is described as the one who hid and fed the prophets of Yahweh (1 Kings 18:4), the hiding place is designated as "the cave," i.e., the well-known cave which comes to mind when Obadiah's name comes up. Likewise, the article used for "the young woman" might indicate "the well-known lady," maybe the queen. Or it might simply be used in a demonstrative sense to refer to a woman in the vicinity of the discussion, thus "that young woman."

As for the question of that female's sexual experience, a word study of 'almāh seems to reveal neutrality on the issue. At Exod. 2:8 the word is used for Moses' young sister about whom we know very little. At Gen. 24:43 the term is used for Rebekah who is described in verse 16 as "a virgin, whom no man had known" (RSV). However, the allusion to Rebekah's sexual inexperience uses, not the word 'almāh, but bᵉtûlāh. Now it is questionable whether even bᵉtûlāh means "virgin," because, if it does, the expression "whom no man had known" is redundant. Finally, 'almāh at Prov. 30:19 seems to refer precisely to a woman who is having sexual experience. The understanding of the woman of Isa. 7:14 as a virgin seems to have originated only when the Hebrew text was translated into Greek; 'almāh then became parthenos which refers to an unmarried girl who apparently is a virgin.

In light of this understanding of 'almāh and on the basis of the definite article, who is "the young woman" who is pregnant? Perhaps no question has enjoyed so much attention among biblical interpreters, but the three most likely candidates are as follows:

(1) Isaiah's wife. The symbolic name "Immanuel" would be quite fitting for the prophet's child, especially since we are told explicitly that Isaiah had two sons with symbolic names: Shear-jashub (7:3) and Maher-shalal-hashbaz (8:3). Of course, it is interesting that, shortly after the statement concerning the birth of a son (7:14), we are told that Isaiah and the prophetess (apparently his wife) had a son. But he was named Maher-shalal-hashbaz and not Immanuel. That Mr. and Mrs. Isaiah would have had two children —one named Immanuel and one named Maher-shalal-hashbaz—in the brief duration of the Syro-Ephraimite alliance is hard to imag-

ISAIAH 7:10–17   113

ine. Thus, while it is *possible* that "*the* young woman" is Isaiah's wife, such an identification is *not probable*.

(2) Ahaz's wife. "*The* young woman" could mean "*the* first lady," although it would be difficult to provide evidence for such a conclusion. At any rate, it is not unlikely that, when Isaiah approached the king with Yahweh's message the second time, others, including the queen, were present. The queen could, indeed, have been pregnant at this time. If she is the young woman in question, then the passage takes on Messianic significance. For the child she bore would be one of the long Davidic line, and such a family tree was essential for the Messiah to come. Moreover, since the Messiah would be a *king* of this Davidic family, the child in the queen's womb would have to be Hezekiah. It was he who succeeded his father in 715 B.C. Thus, Hezekiah would have been born with the symbolic name Immanuel and would have been hailed as the expected deliverer. Perhaps it is his birth which is announced so joyously at Isa. 9:6–7. When it is realized that Hezekiah, during his reign, made some startling moves to free Judah from Assyrian domination and to purify the temple at Jerusalem (2 Kings 18:3–8), one can imagine the optimism and confidence of the people in their celebrated "Messiah."

However, there is one serious problem with this entire theory. The whole notion rests on the concept that Hezekiah was the child in the womb while the Syro-Ephraimite alliance threatened Judah in 734 B.C. According to 2 Kings 18:2, however, Hezekiah was twenty-five years old when he came to the throne. Since the year of his accession was 715, he must have been born in 740 B.C., six years before the circumstances of our text. Of course, it is possible that the Deuteronomistic historian who wrote 2 Kings 18:2 was wrong about the young king's age; he is known to have made some errors in his chronology. However, at the present time the evidence falls against the Messianic/Hezekiah interpretation.

(3) Any unidentified pregnant woman in eyesight of the king and Isaiah. "*The* young woman" could mean "that young lady over there who is pregnant."[3]

---

3. It is the position of Otto Kaiser, *Isaiah 1–12*, pp. 96–106, that "the young woman" refers generally to many pregnant girls in the land who, upon the birth of sons, will rejoice by naming their children Immanuel.

After all this discussion, it is clear that the young lady cannot be identified with any certainty. But, further, it is obvious that unless the woman is the queen, it does not really matter who she is. In other words, the passage has Messianic significance only if the woman is Ahaz's wife and if the son-to-be-born is Hezekiah. Apart from that possibility, the emphasis lies on the birth of a child in the near future, whose name Immanuel signifies the presence of God in the midst of the people and the end to the present threat.

Verse 15: The "curds and honey" in this verse and in the following is variously interpreted. Most commentators argue that it is a menu for basic sustenance, one which designates a time of poverty following disaster. Usually verses 21–22 are cited to show what men will eat after the destruction of the land described in verses 18–20. But once again, a concordance is a necessary tool. How are curds and honey used elsewhere in the Old Testament? Apart from Isa. 7:15, 22, this same combination of food items occurs elsewhere only at 2 Sam. 17:29 and at Job 20:17. In the former passage, curds and honey are among the items brought to David at Mahanayim. It could be argued that these foods for basic sustenance were delivered to David who was "camping out" during his son's takeover of the palace; it could also be argued, however, that curds and honey were the delicacies brought to the king along with beds, basins, wheat, meal, grains, beans, and lentils (2 Sam. 17:28). Such a list of goodies does not seem to indicate that David and his men were roughing it. At Job 20:17 the situation is clearer: curds and honey are signs of prosperity which are denied to the godless man.

Apart from the combination, "curds" alone appears as a food of prosperity at Job 29:6, Gen. 18:18, Deut. 32:14, Judg. 5:25. Furthermore, even Isa. 7:22 speaks of an "abundance" which the remnant will have to eat. Thus, the use of a concordance turns up the indication that a time of prosperity will prevail by the time the child "knows to refuse what is harmful and to choose what is good." But when does a child make that distinction?

Verses 15–16: "What is harmful . . . and what is good." The combination of good and harmful can mean several different things: (a) moral alternatives (see Deut. 1:39; Ps. 34:14; Prov. 31:12; Amos 5:14–15; Mic. 3:2); (b) "everything" (see Gen.

2:9, 17; 3:5, 22); (c) pleasant and unpleasant food (see 2 Sam. 19:35). Which of these possibilities is intended by the author is difficult to determine. The use of good and harmful as "everything," i.e., omniscience, is possible if the child is the Messiah who would be endowed with special gifts of wisdom and understanding (see Isa. 11:2). Apart from a Messianic interpretation of the passage, however, the concept of omniscience is not possible. If (a) moral alternatives are intended, then the child would have to be at least several years old. But if (c) the distinction between pleasant and unpleasant food is meant, then the child need be only hours old.

It seems that the time of prosperity to come (our conclusion upon studying "curds and honey") will occur shortly after the birth of a child who is already in the womb or a few years after his birth. Or, least likely, when the heir to the throne succeeds his father. At any rate, the solution to the impending crisis is near at hand.

Verse 17: The preceding statement implies a positive, rather than a negative, interpretation of "days which have not come since the turning aside of Ephraim from Judah." Such "days" would then be the glorious days of the Davidic/Solomonic empire *before* the northern kingdom broke away from Judah in the reign of Rehoboam.

"The king of Assyria," attached loosely at the end of this verse, makes no sense at all. The phrase should probably be omitted, as it seems to be a scribal error. *NEB*, in fact, does omit the phrase entirely.

4. THE CRITICISMS

The discussion of literary matters raised the question concerning the *form* of the passage, for several characteristics of the announcement of judgment which we examined at Mic. 3:9–12 are evident in this passage as well. The *introduction* "Listen, O house of David!" is quite similar to the summons to hear at Mic. 3:9. The *accusation* here, given as a *reason* for judgment, appears in the form of the question of verse 13. The *messenger formula* is obvious in the "therefore" of verse 14, and the *announcement of judgment* would be developed by the *intervention of God* ("the

Lord himself will give you a sign") and by the *results of intervention* which would consider "curds and honey" (verse 15) as a poverty diet and the "such days" of verse 17 as a disaster equal to the
splitting of the monarchy under Rehoboam.

Thus, form-critically the passage seems to be an announcement
of judgment. Such a classification conflicts, however, with the
results of the word study on "curds and honey" which led to the
conclusion that the pronouncement is one of salvation. How then is
the passage to be interpreted? First of all, we must seek to discover
how Isaiah himself uses "signs" elsewhere in his preaching. At Isa.
37:30–31 the "sign" points to a period of famine which will be
followed in the third year by a situation in which the people flour-
ish and harvest their own food. At Isa. 7:1–9, Isaiah's son, Shear-
jashub ("A remnant shall return"), is a positive sign as the Lord
announces to Ahaz the coming failure of the alliance against him.

It may be, then, that the prophet Isaiah intended his message to
be one of judgment *and* of salvation. He may have used the typical
form of announcement of judgment to speak the Lord's displeasure
at the king's lack of faith and the inevitability of disaster which
follows. At the same time, he filled that form with a content which
proclaimed that days of prosperity for the people, the continuation
of the dynasty, and a restoration of stability lay in the not-too-dis-
tant future. In this way God would remain faithful to his promise
issued to David centuries earlier. Isaiah was proclaiming, in other
words, that God's promise continues in spite of the shortcomings
of men.

The *tradition* of Isa. 7:10–17, especially verse 14, is precisely
what has made this passage one of the most popular texts in the
entire Old Testament. The use of 7:14 at Matt. 1:23 serves as a
prophecy for the virgin birth of Jesus. Since this birth story immediately follows the genealogy of Matt. 1:1–17 which establishes
the Davidic line of Jesus, the quotation points also to the Messianic role which this Christ-child was to play. This use of the quotation by Matthew, however, is somewhat different from the use in
Isaiah 7. In the Old Testament passage, the name Immanuel is to
be the name of the child; at Matt. 1:23 the name is a symbolic
Messianic title applied to the child whose actual name is to be
Jesus.

At any rate, on the basis of our exegesis of Isa. 7:10–17, we have seen that the passage does not point to the birth of Jesus seven hundred years off in the future. Rather it speaks of an immediate situation in the lifetime of Isaiah, one which will come to pass in the birth and maturity of a child who is already in his mother's womb. But because the name Immanuel means "God with us," and because the Septuagint version which Matthew used rendered *'almāh* as "virgin," the passage was used as a prophecy of Christ. Thus, the passage was taken out of its context and original meaning and reinterpreted in light of the person of Christ.

5. Context

It has already been made clear that the passage must be interpreted in light of the preceding section in 7:1–9 and in the larger context of Isa. 6:1–9:6 which seems to originate just prior to and in the midst of the Syro-Ephraimite crisis.

6. Interpretative Rendering

Again the Lord spoke to Ahaz concerning the attempt of Ephraim and Syria to replace the king with the non-Davidic son of Tabeel. When Ahaz hypocritically refused the sign of God's faithfulness to his promise of an enduring Davidic dynasty, Isaiah rebuked him with judgment but gave the sign anyway. The sign was this: "That young woman standing near us, the pregnant one, will bear a son whom she will name 'God with us.' When he is old enough to distinguish unpleasant tastes from pleasant ones (or to make moral decisions), he shall be eating the food of prosperous times. For before he reaches that age, Ephraim and Syria, who have made you so anxious, will be devastated. The Lord will bring upon this land of Judah days of glory such as we have not seen since the majestic reign of Solomon."

7. Theology of the Passage

In the light of the total situation in history, the form-critical analysis of the passage, and the word study on "curds and honey," Isaiah's proclamation can be summed up as follows: *In the midst of and in spite of man's stubborn attempts to establish his own security, God renews his promise that he alone will make his people secure.*

When this theological statement comes into contact with that of the Christian interpreter, there is obvious a consistency or continuity between the witnesses of the two Testaments. The Father of Jesus Christ comes judging us when we, his redeemed people to whom have been given the promises, attempt to launch out on our own without him and without regard to his faithfulness to us. In fact, it is precisely in our attempts to establish our own security that we can be convicted of works-righteousness on the one hand, or libertinism, on the other. In either case we are asserting our independence of the God who came in his Son to do it all for us. And yet, in spite of this asserted independence, in spite of our attempt to be prodigal sons, God the Father invites us to rely on him and to trust his Word. Thus, while the passage at Isa. 7:10–17 is not a prediction about Jesus' birth, it does proclaim a witness which we see fulfilled decisively in the Christ event. In this way the passage has importance for homiletics even if we do not use it as Matthew did.[4]

4. For further theological implications of the passage, see Otto Kaiser, *Isaiah 1–12*, pp. 105–106.

Isaiah

6:1–8 (13)

1. Establishing a Working Text
A comparison of some English translations

Since a literal rendering of the Hebrew in this passage does not contribute any elements which do not occur in the translations used, a translation of my own is not presented here. The problems with the text center on the following points of comparison:

Verse 3: *AV*: ". . . the whole earth *is* full of his glory!"
        RSV: ". . . the whole earth is full of his glory."
        NEB: ". . . the whole earth is full of his glory."
        Kaiser: ". . . his glory is the fullness of the whole earth."

The rendering by Kaiser is identical to the construction and syntax of the Hebrew. The translation of the other three seems to indicate that God's glory is *in* the world, but the literal rendering of the Hebrew (followed by Kaiser) seems to announce that the world in some way *is* his glory.

Verse 5: *AV*: "Woe is me! for I am undone; . . ."
        RSV: "Woe is me! For I am lost; . . ."
        NEB: "Woe is me! I am lost, . . ."
        Kaiser: "Woe is me; for I must be silent, . . ."

Again Kaiser's translation differs from the others; the problem here lies in the meaning of the Hebrew verb which will be discussed below.

Verse 5: *AV*: "for mine eyes have seen the King, the Lord of hosts."

> RSV: "for my eyes have seen the King, the Lord of hosts!"
>
> NEB: "yet with these eyes I have seen the King, the Lord of Hosts."
>
> Kaiser: "For my eyes have seen the King, Yahweh Sebaoth."

While here and in verse 3 Kaiser transliterates Yahweh Sebaoth rather than translates it as "the Lord of Hosts," the major difference is NEB'S "yet" rather than the usual "for." The translation "for" of the Hebrew *kî* explains the reason for Isaiah's devastation at the beginning of the verse, but NEB's "yet" indicates that Isaiah has seen the Lord in spite of his and his people's sinfulness.

> Verse 8: AV: "... and who will go for us?"
>
> RSV: "... and who will go for us?"
>
> NEB: "Who will go for me?"
>
> Kaiser: "... and who will go from us?"

The obvious difficulty with the literal translation of the last word "us" is the identity of the audience about whom Yahweh is speaking. NEB smooths out the difficulty by translating it in the singular.

2. LITERARY MATTERS

These eight verses may provide more significant testimony than any other such block of material in the Old Testament. The passage is "loaded" with almost too much significance for a brief study such as this. For the sake of brevity and clarity, therefore, our treatment will fail to do justice to the full depth and breadth of the text, but we shall, in our selectivity, try to pick out enough for comment in order to provide some means for interpretation.

The authorship of this passage is universally assigned to Isaiah. The autobiographical account is quite understandable in terms of the style and content of other Isaianic material. Furthermore, the passage even provides a precise date: "the year that King Uzziah died," any history of Israel or commentator will explain, was probably 742 B.C. We are not told whether this call of Isaiah took place before or after the king's death in that year, but the superscription to the book at 1:1 (probably added by a later editor) gives the impression that some of Isaiah's ministry came *during* the reign of Uzziah. At any rate, Isaiah's prophetic experience occurred shortly before the Syro-Ephraimite crisis of the following decade and is included in the block of material in 6:1 to 9:7 which dates from that general time rather than at the beginning of the book where we would expect to find such a call recorded.

Verse 1: The vision took place in the temple, perhaps during an annual festival event when the Ark was carried from the Holy of Holies to some other location. The description of the "king's" train here seems to indicate that an entourage was moving out of or into the elevated platform of the Holy of Holies which housed the Ark where the Lord sat enthroned. It is equally possible, however, that Isaiah's description is purely visionary and has little, if anything, to do with an actual liturgical procession. The vision could have occurred, in other words, on any day in which Isaiah was at worship in the temple. What is interesting, at any rate, is that while Isaiah says he "saw" the Lord, the description he gives concerns everything around him rather than the Lord himself.

Verse 2: That Yahweh is surrounded by creatures in his court is attested elsewhere in the Old Testament; see 1 Kings 22:19 ff.; Job 1.

Verse 3: The song of praise these strange looking seraphim (whatever they are!) were calling to one another is a beautiful expression of God's *holiness* and *glory*. These two words are important to understand, and a Bible dictionary can serve this purpose well. The Old Testament view of holiness means basically "separateness"; that which is holy is that which is set aside from profane use or set apart for particular, usually cultic, use. To speak of God's holiness is to bear witness to his transcendence, to his "otherness," from man and from the world. The word *glory* means basically "weight, heaviness, power." It is used of men who are rich and influential, who "throw their weight around." Thus, glory has to do with a manifestation of someone's power or influence, that by which a man is known. The use of the word *glory* in reference to God has a particularly interesting development, especially in the works of Ezekiel and the Priest. But perhaps it is sufficient at this point to note that God's glory is elsewhere associated with the temple and the Ark before the days of Ezekiel and P (1 Sam.

4:21–22; Pss. 24:7–10; 63:2; 78:61), and so the emphasis on glory in Isaiah's temple vision is almost to be expected.

What is interesting in the hymn of the seraphim, however, is that while the first line testifies to the separateness or transcendence of God (his holiness), the second line indicates that his power and influence are manifested not only in but also *as* the created world (his glory). While God is distinct, he is also manifest to men. This hymn might be one of the most powerful theological statements that can be made today concerning our despoiled earth.

As for the origin and meaning of the title "the Lord of hosts," there has been much debate. It has been explained as referring to the Lord of the heavenly armies, of Israel's army, or of all divinities whom the pagans worship. Other scholars have argued that since the name *Yahweh* is never elsewhere used in the sense of "Yahweh of" (Hebrew construct state), the word *hosts* must be in apposition to Yahweh meaning "Yahweh, the sum total of powers." Whatever the ultimate answer to this question might be, it is significant for us to note that the title is usually related to the Ark of the Covenant (see especially 1 Sam. 4:4) and thus confirms the whole vision as taking place in the temple and looking toward the Holy of Holies.

Verse 4: The presence of smoke and the quaking of the earth are typical of "theophanies" (God-appearances). We shall return to this matter under our discussion of form-criticism.

Verse 5: The distinction among the translations cited above has to do, first of all, with whether the Hebrew word is *dāmāh*="to cease, to destroy" (and thus in the passive [*niph ʿal*] "I am lost" or "I am undone") or *dāmam*="to be silent." Clearly, the former root is that which appears in the Hebrew text as pointed by the Masoretes; to argue for the latter root requires a very slight emendation. However, as it turns out in this case, even the latter word, when used in the passive (*niph ʿal*) stem, as it is here, means "to be made silent," i.e., "to be destroyed." Thus, in either case, the meaning is basically the same, and Kaiser's translation "I must be silent" is misleading.

What lies behind the whole meaning of Isaiah's "woe" is the notion that, when man looks at God who is "other," the observer will die. There exists such a qualitative difference between the transcendent God and sinful man that man cannot withstand the encounter (see Exod. 33:20; Judg. 13:22, and the surprise of Jacob that he remained alive at Gen. 32:30). With this understanding, the reading "*for* my eyes have seen" is to be preferred over *NEB*'s "yet."

Verse 8: After God had cleansed Isaiah of his sin, the Lord asked, "Whom shall I send, and who will go for *us*?" *NEB*'s "for *me*" certainly avoids the problem, but it does some injustice to the literal "from *us*." To whom and about whom is the Lord speaking when he says "us"? Such statements from God occur also at Gen. 1:26: "Let *us* make man in *our* image . . ."; Gen. 3:22: "Behold, the man has become like one of *us* . . ."; Gen. 11:4: "Come, let *us* go down and confuse their language. . . ." Such divine plurals (my italics) in the first person have been interpreted in a number of ways: (1) as an editorial "we"; (2) as a plural of majesty; (3) as a reference to heavenly beings of some sort who are present in the Lord's court. While the second possibility is very real, the third seems to be intended in our passage because such courtiers have already been mentioned: the seraphim. Furthermore, it has been pointed out above that at 1 Kings 22:19 ff. and Job 1, God is indeed portrayed as surrounded by and addressing his court.

Isaiah's response "Here I am!" is identical to the response of others who are summoned by God for a particular task. It is the response of Abraham when he is asked to sacrifice Isaac (Gen. 22:1), of Moses when he is commanded to bring the Hebrew slaves out of Egypt (Exod. 3:4), and of Samuel when he is told to serve as a messenger to Eli (1 Sam. 3:2 ff.). In each of these cases, the person involved is addressed by name, but in our text Isaiah, overwhelmed at the experience of the presence of a holy but forgiving God, responds as though he were personally addressed by God's question. And indeed he was!

The passage listed in the lectionary consists of verses 1-8. However, the passage obviously continues as far as verse 13. In fact, the account is incomplete without that speech, for in verses 9-13 is given the content and the purpose of Isaiah's call. He is to speak God's Word so that the people's hearts will be hardened and in this way bring God's judgment on Judah. Isaiah's call is one of the most difficult passages to comprehend, for he is called to be a failure: to speak God's Word clearly and forthrightly so that the people will reject it and bring devastation upon themselves. But in spite of its difficulty, the speech of God in verses 9–13 must be regarded within the scope of the passage, for without this content God calls a prophet who is given no message. Such an omission is impossible to understand in light of prophetic theology.

3. SETTING IN LIFE

The historical allusion to the year of Uzziah's death sets the passage at about 742 B.C. It was a time of impending disaster on the international scene, for Tiglath-Pileser III, king of the ever-expanding Assyrian Empire, had the kingdoms of Palestine shaking in their boots. Takeover of the whole area by this brilliant military leader was inevitable, and the Assyrians were well known for their brutality and ruthlessness. As Isaiah's preaching developed, the Assyrian kings were interpreted as Yahweh's instruments of judgment upon his people, and so the judgment which this prophet preached, though it was Yahweh's Word and command, would come at the hands of the Assyrians (see especially Isa. 10:5–11).

The eighth century B.C. was also a time of prophetic denunciation of the evils of society, especially of the oppression of the weak by the strong and rich. This sociological situation, described more fully in connection with Mic. 3:9–12, was a theological problem for the redeemed and elected people of God.

4. THE CRITICISMS

The text can be classified according to several forms—depending upon which verses or characteristics are emphasized. To begin with, the passage in verses 1–8 is a narrative, and the first verse makes clear that the narrative is a visionary account. But since the vision is of God, the passage can be classified as a *theophany*.

The designation of the passage as a theophany brings to mind several other theophany texts in the Old Testament: Exod. 19:16–19; 20:18; 24:9–11; Ps. 18:7–15; Job 37; Ezek. 1:4–28. What is characteristic of such theophanies is the presence of thunder and lightning, earthquake, and smoke. But what is even more striking in these texts is that God is never described; while the individuals or the people "see" the Lord, only the signs of his presence are designated. In this respect, theophanies in the Old Testament differ from theophanies of other ancient Near Eastern peoples who both described and portrayed their gods. Moreover, in almost all such "theophanies" in the Old Testament (with the exception of Exod. 24:9-11 and Ps. 18:7-15), the texts move directly from the descriptive signs of his presence to God speaking to the man or men intended. Thus the emphasis is *not* on the vision but on what God says. The same is true of our text at Isa. 6:1-8. While the beginning of the passage deals with a theophanic description (court creatures, earthquake, thunder, and smoke) and with Isaiah's awe before these signs (like the people at Exod. 19:16-19; 20:18; like Job at Job 41:6; and like Ezek. at 1:28), the text moves on to its climax with the Lord's address to Isaiah concerning the message he is to speak.

Since the climax of the text is the calling of Isaiah to be a messenger and the message he is to proclaim, then the passage can more appropriately be called a *report of a prophetic call*, similar to those at Jer. 1:4-10 and Ezek. 2:1-3:16. In Chapter Four of Part One, a brief comparison of these reports was made as an illustration of a prophetic form. It was stated there that the purpose of these reports was to provide authenticity for the preaching of these men as messengers of Yahweh. While Ezekiel was a priest and Jeremiah of priestly origin and training, Isaiah's prior activity is unknown to us. In all cases, however, the report of their calls legitimizes their role as prophets since apparently none of them was officially installed as a cultic prophet (see also Amos 7:14-15).

In comparing and contrasting these three reports, several emphases stand out in Isaiah's call which are not present in the other two: the incident takes place in the temple; the overwhelming presence causes Isaiah to confess his and his people's sin from which he is forgiven; Isaiah volunteers for the task once he has been cleansed; and, above all, Isaiah's preaching is solely to hasten the judgment of God, for it is clear that God's mind is already made up. Thus, employing the category of a prophetic call report, Isaiah has made some peculiar emphases which are important for the interpretation of this passage.

As for the *tradition-critical* aspects of the passage, there are two notes worthy of mention, and both have to do with the message which Isaiah was to proclaim. First, Isaiah was apparently using an old tradition which has been called the "hardness-of-heart motif." Gerhard von Rad has demonstrated that this motif, as difficult as it is to understand, was inherited by Isaiah from old traditions in Israel and in the ancient world as a whole. In the Old Testament Yahweh's hardening of men's hearts is attested in such old traditions as 1 Kings 22:21; Judg. 9:23; 1 Sam. 16:14; 18:10; 19:9; 2 Sam. 17:14; 1 Kings 12:15; and, of course, in the exodus story in reference to the heart of Pharaoh. But Isaiah used this old motif to announce Israel's downfall (see also Isa. 29:9–14) and to point beyond the coming disaster to a saving event (see 6:13), both understood as the result of the creative Word of Yahweh. Thus, in the use of this motif, as in several others, Isaiah reinterprets an old tradition to say something unique about God's activity with his people.[1]

Second, the message which Isaiah is commissioned to preach to the people is used in several ways by New Testament writers. In the Synoptic Gospels (Matt. 13:14–15; Mark 4:12; Luke 8:10) the hardness-of-heart motif of Isa. 6:9–10 is used as the explanation for Jesus' use of parables in his teaching. The precise meaning of this explanation for parables has been debated, but it seems that the intention is to announce to the disciples that only those so elected understand the meaning behind the parables; to others they remain only simple stories ("they hear but they do not understand"). At Mark 8:17–18 the same passage from Isaiah is alluded to as an address against the disciples who did not understand the meaning of Jesus' act of feeding the multitudes. The use of the motif in connection with the failure to understand Jesus' acts as signs of something beyond the appearance can be seen also at John 12:36b–41 where the quotation speaks of the unbelieving multitudes. Finally, Paul, frustrated by the disbelief of the Jews in his message about the kingdom of God and about Jesus, quotes the passage as having been fulfilled and thus uses it as the reason for his mission to the Gentiles (Acts 28:23–28).

It is clear, then, that the message of our text in verses 9–13, especially that of verses 9–10, was more important in the tradition

1. See Gerhard von Rad, *Old Testament Theology*, vol. II, trans. D. M. G. Stalker (New York: Harper & Row, 1965), pp. 151–155.

of the passage than the vision which preceded it. This use of the tradition confirms what was said earlier under the discussion of form: even in the so-called theophanies of the Old Testament the emphasis is not on the vision but on the message to be proclaimed. Such a conclusion might encourage a lector to read beyond the designated pericope which ends at verse 8. It should also play an important role in the sermon which develops from this passage.

5. CONTEXT

In this case, as was true also of Isa. 7:10–17, the question of context cannot be separated from the material in 6:1–9:6 which originates from Isaiah himself and dates from the same general period (742–34 B.C.). Also, once again, while chapter 6 is an independent report, the message or the theology contained therein must be interpreted in light of Isaiah's preaching as a whole. For this overview of that prophet's theology, a good commentary or general introduction or even an article in a Bible dictionary will serve well.

6. INTERPRETATIVE RENDERING

In the year that Uzziah died, 742 B.C., while at worship in the temple at Jerusalem, the Lord appeared to me with all the signs of his splendor. The impact of his presence drove home to me my own unworthiness and that of the people among whom I live. But the Lord, through one of his mediating courtiers, forgave my sin and then asked for a volunteer to serve him. I responded as a man does when summoned by the Lord and volunteered for his service. Then he told me what it was that he wanted me to say: "Speak my Word clearly and forthrightly with the result that the people will reject my Word and bring upon themselves the judgment I have already decreed." I was aghast at the thought of such a mission, and so I asked how long I must speak. The Lord answered that my mission would continue until he had brought utter devastation on the land. This is the story of how I came to be a prophet—not through the official laying on of hands in a cultic ceremony, not through familial tradition, but through the devastating and comforting presence of the Lord who gave me the message that I preach.

7. THEOLOGIES OF THE PASSAGE

Though we are dealing here with a unit which probably goes back to the prophet himself with little, if any, editorial revision, there are several important proclamations which can be heard from this passage. In the first seven verses the proclamation seems to be: *In the presence of the holy God who drives men to their knees, that same God acts to forgive sin and bridge the gulf between them.* Such a proclamation, though it does not give full justice to the purpose of the account by Isaiah, is certainly consistent with the New Testament understanding of the power of God's presence and of his will to accept men in spite of themselves.

As indicated above, however, the purpose of the account by Isaiah is to record his call to be God's messenger and, particularly, the content of the message he was to proclaim. In this way the theology of the text can be summarized as: *To those who are judged and then forgiven by the presence of God and his Word, God gives a mission to be spokesmen of that Word—no matter how incomprehensible and difficult that Word might be.* Again, from a Christian perspective such a proclamation is not only useful but imperative, for all who stand judged and justified by God's act on the cross are given precisely that scandalous message to proclaim.

Finally, but still not exhausting the text's possibilities, an emphasis in Isaiah's call, which is not in those of Jeremiah or Ezekiel, is that his summons occurs while he is at worship. This point can lead to the proclamation: *In the midst of liturgical routine God comes to devastate, to comfort, and to lead those who hear his Word addressing them.* This rather comprehensive interpretation of the passage requires little imagination to see how it could be addressed to a Christian congregation for whom Christ is present in the words—all too familiar, it seems—of the liturgy, the reading of the biblical lessons, the sermon, and the sacraments.

1 Kings

19:9–18

1. Establishing a Working Text

There is little to be gained in presenting here the literal translation of this passage or even in making an extensive comparison of English translations. In setting side by side *RSV*, *NEB*, and John Gray's translation[1] it is clear that only one major difference occurs in the passage, and that occurs in verse 12 at the description of the "voice":

> *RSV*: "... and after the fire a still small voice."
> *NEB*: "... and after the fire a low murmuring sound."
> Gray: "... and after the fire a sound of thin silence."

Gray's translation is a quite literal one which I would change only slightly to "and after the fire the sound of crushed silence." The obvious difference in meaning between *RSV* and the others is that the former intends to describe an audible and apparently communicable voice while the others range from a slight noise of some sort (*NEB*) to a poetic way of describing absolute silence (Gray).

No other significant differences occur in the comparison of these three English translations, but the Hebrew has the definite article in verse 9 "the cave" rather than the English translations' rendering as "a cave."

Keeping in mind these two matters, the interpreter can use any one of the above translations as a working text.

---

1. *I & II Kings*, "The Old Testament Library" (Philadelphia: Westminster Press, 1963), p. 362.

2. LITERARY MATTERS

The Books of Kings make up the last portion of the so-called Deuteronomistic history which includes as well Deuteronomy, Joshua, Judges, and Samuel. While there is some debate as to the time of this Deuteronomistic school, it does seem that the work of these writers was carried out sometime after 560 B.C. (the date of the last detail recorded at 2 Kings 25:27–30). Furthermore, it seems that these historians/editors did their massive work in Babylon and addressed it to the exiles there. It is clear that the Deuteronomists inherited and used large blocks of already existing material: stories about the judges, the court history of David, the succession narrative of Solomon, chronicles of the kings of Israel and of Judah, and legends about prophets. In some cases the Deuteronomists did little to the works they inherited; in other cases they edited material freely. And so, our passage belongs to the legends of Elijah which were handed down to the exilic historians; it may or may not have some of their editorial comments which give us the present form of the story.

Verse 9: "there." The previous verse makes clear that the adverb refers to Horeb, the mount of God. It is clear from the Book of Deuteronomy and elsewhere that Horeb is another name for Sinai. One need only read Deut. 4:1–11:32 to see that everything that happened at Sinai in Exod. 19–34 is said to have occurred at Horeb. Thus Horeb is the Deuteronomist's term for Sinai.

Verse 9: "the cave." Since a cave has not been mentioned in the preceding paragraph, the definite article here cannot mean "the aforementioned cave." Moreover, since the teller of the story does not seem to be standing in the vicinity of the cave, the article does not mean "that cave yonder." The article can only mean "*the* cave" or "the well-known cave." Since we are discussing a particular cave on Mount Sinai/Horeb, "the cave" must be the one familiar to the people from the story about God's appearance to Moses who was stationed in "a cleft of the rock" (Exod. 33:17–23).

Verse 11: "Stand on the mount before the Lord" and "the Lord passed by." Both of these expressions, particularly in light of the mountain as Sinai and on the basis of identifying the old familiar cave, are reminiscent of the story at Exod. 33:17–23 where Moses was told to stand on (or by) the rock as the Lord "passes by."

Verse 12: "a sound of crushed silence." Unfortunately, no comparable expression occurs elsewhere in the Old Testament, and so a word study is impossible. While the translation "sound of . . . silence" seems contradictory, it probably is a rather poetic way of describing absolute silence, a vacuum of sound, which is crushing in its impact on Elijah. This silence stands in sharp contrast to the scene which preceded it.

Verse 14 (and the end of 13): The repetition of the Lord's question "What are you doing here, Elijah?" and the prophet's self-righteous response (first occurring at verses 9–10) is often regarded as an error, an unnecessary repetition due to a scribe's mistake (dittography). However, the repetition may indeed be intentional by the author in order to emphasize something or to make a special point.

Verse 14: "your covenant." The word *covenant* is one of the most important terms in the Old Testament. Its use and development can be traced through an article in a Bible dictionary (to use Kittel's *Theological Dictionary of the New Testament*, look up *diatehēkē* in Volume IV). It is sufficient to point out here that, while "covenant" refers to a relationship in which God obligates himself (to Abraham at Gen. 15:12–21; 17:1–21; to David at 2 Samuel 7), it is also used of a relationship in which God puts the obligation on his redeemed people (Exodus 20–23). The use of the word *covenant* in verses 10 and 14 of our text can only refer to that Sinai covenant in which God set the rules for his people to live—rules which they broke in throwing down Yahweh's altars in order to worship Baal.

Verses 15–16: "anoint." The term is worth a sentence or so here simply because the word *māšăh* is that which becomes Messiah, "the anointed one." That the term is used here for anointing kings and prophets signifies that the act of anointing designates someone or something for a particular task. A Bible dictionary is helpful for a summary of the uses of the word.

3. SETTING IN LIFE

Elijah was active as a prophet in the northern kingdom of Israel during the second quarter of the ninth century B.C. The dynasty of Omri was still in power in the person of Ahab who, in order to establish some political ties, was married to Jezebel, a Phoenician and the daughter of the king of Tyre. Jezebel's presence in Israel's royal city of Samaria brought to a head the failure of the people of Israel to distinguish between Baal and Yahweh. Jezebel had her prophets of Baal and of Asherah who sat at the queen's table (1 Kings 18:19). The people, some offended by pagan worship in Israel and some impressed by it, were caught in a syncretistic situation in which they could no longer decide which god to worship (see 1 Kings 18:21). This struggle provided Elijah's reason for being; his very name "Yahu (Yahweh) is my God" describes his function in the life of Israel. His contest with the prophets of Baal on Mount Carmel (1 Kings 18:20–40) was his triumph in demonstrating the power of Yahweh over that of Baal. But for slaughtering Jezebel's prophets after that triumph, Elijah was in serious trouble, and so fled to save his life.

4. THE CRITICISMS

The story before us is, of course, a narrative about an incident in the life of a prophet. Since it deals with a holy man at a holy place, the narrative might be classified as a *legend*. However, unlike the story of Elijah with the widow of Zarephath (1 Kings 17) or the many feats attributed to the prophet Elisha, this story has nothing about it which is complimentary for Elijah. It does not seem to portray him as a legendary figure. As for the holy place as a means for classifying the narrative as a legend, we shall postpone judgment on that issue until further investigation is made.

On the basis of the mention of wind, earthquake, and fire, some might classify the account as a *theophany*. These elements, typical of theophanic descriptions at Exod. 19:16–19; 20:18; Job 37; Isaiah 6:1–4, etc., play an important role in our story. However, just as the negative is more than a curiosity in the prohibitions of the Ten Commandments, so the word *not* here is essential to the understanding of the passage. Since the Lord was *not* in the wind, earthquake, or fire, the passage is precisely *not* a theophany. In fact, the narrator is so explicit about God's absence in these phenomena that we might call the story a polemic against theophany theology. In this way, the situation of Elijah is highlighted: unlike the Baals of Canaan who are identified with the phenomena of powerful natural forces, Yahweh is Lord over nature but in no way is identical to or identifiable with such phenomena. Here is clearly an attempt to distinguish Yahwistic theology from that of the Canaanite worship of Baal. That distinction, we have already seen, was Elijah's mission in ninth-century Israel. Thus, however we classify the story in regard to form, the basic intention or proclamation of the story seems to be: *Unlike the gods of Canaan Yahweh is not to be found in the natural phenomena usually associated with theophanies.* Such a proclamation is, of course, purely negative, and one must immediately ask, Where then is he to be found? The text seems to indicate that *he is not to be found at all; rather he comes to men speaking his Word* (verse 9, verses 15–18). He comes to Elijah in his Word which sends the prophet off on a mission to anoint kings and a prophetic successor. Yahweh is thus portrayed as a God of history rather than a God of nature.

We have already begun a discussion of *tradition criticism.* In the narratives at Exod. 19:16–19; 20:18; 24:9–11; and above all at 33:17–23, Sinai is indeed a place of theophany. Men see God (24:10–11) or his back (33:23) or at least the signs of his presence (19:16–19; 20:18) on Sinai. The story told about Sinai, alias Horeb, at 1 Kings 19:9–18, however, completely rejects the idea that Sinai is a place of theophany. In fact, as we saw above, our story is told in such a way as to call attention deliberately to the theophany before Moses at Exod. 33:17–23 which took place on the mount, at a (the) cave, where the Lord passed by. Moses saw God (at least his back) says the old tradition, but the new tradition tells us that God was *not* seen by Elijah. Rather God used an audio-visual demonstration to show Elijah that he was *not* to be found or seen, even on the famous holy mountain. The old Sinai tradition has been radically reinterpreted, and this reinterpretation explains the repeated use of the Lord's question to Elijah: "What are you doing *here?*" Elijah, not understanding the question, explained to God that he sought refuge on the holy mountain where Yahweh was present. God's response to that speech was the demonstration that he was *not* there on the mountain any more or any less than he was present in the cities and countryside below. But when God asked the question again, Elijah gave the same speech. He did not understand the point of the non-verbal demonstration, and so God clearly communicated to the prophet by his Word which directed Elijah to leave the mountain and to do God's work "down there where the action is."

The sacred mountain is thereby desacralized by drawing intentional parallels to the earlier Sinai theophanies. How much of this reinterpretation belongs to the basic or original story directed against Baal worship is difficult to say. But it is quite possible, perhaps even probable, that the story, precisely as we have it, is the result of some editorial work by the Deuteronomists. Simply by supplying the name Horeb and by wording verses 9–11 in such a way as to call attention to the story of Moses on Sinai/Horeb, the Deuteronomists seem to have desacralized the mountain in order to proclaim: *Far from confining himself in holy places where men must come to meet him, God comes to men in his Word, sending them into the midst of historical events.*

Such a proclamation is typical of the Deuteronomists and crucial for the situation they were addressing. It would have been theological suicide to maintain the sacredness of places and objects to exiles in Babylon whose temple with its Ark back in Jerusalem had been demolished years earlier. Indeed, if God were confined to mountains, temples, and thrones, then God was dead, or at least unreachable from Babylon. And so, for the Deuteronomists, God chooses the temple for his name to dwell (Deut. 12:5, 11, and often), but God himself lives in heaven (Deut. 26:15). In this way the Deuteronomists not only reinterpreted the name of God (the view that the name *is* the person now is changed to the notion that the name is God's means of relating to his people), they also reinterpreted the significance of the temple. As for the Ark which in the old tradition was the throne on which Yahweh sat enthroned (1 Sam. 4:4; Num. 10:35–36), this cultic object becomes for the Deuteronomists nothing more than a box which contained the tablets of the law (Deut. 10:1–5). Thus, the Deuteronomists reinterpreted several old sacral traditions in order to emphasize the presence of God in his Word, for only in this way could the exiles experience his presence in far-off Babylon after the destruction of the temple and in a captive situation which prevented them from making pilgrimages to Sinai. Here indeed is a dynamic witness to the Word of God which addresses men in new situations in new and different ways.

5. CONTEXT

Set after the incident at Mount Carmel where Elijah had the prophets of Baal killed, the journey to Horeb is seen as the attempt of the prophet to find security in a holy place. We have already seen that God sent him back into the midst of the turmoil with some specific functions to perform. Thus the context serves to confirm some of the interpretation described above. But the combination of this context with the announcement that God will leave a remnant in Israel (verse 18) gives a slightly different meaning to the story: *In the midst of men's anxieties over doing the Lord's work, God announces that while he constantly sends men out to perform his will, the present and the future are nevertheless in his hands.*

6. INTERPRETATIVE RENDERING

[9]And there, on the mountain of God, Horeb (also known as Sinai), Elijah entered the old familiar cave which we all know from the story about Moses, and there he spent the night. And lo, the Word of the Lord came to him saying, "What are you doing *here*, Elijah?" . . . [12]. . . and after the fire, absolute silence. [13]And when Elijah heard this vacuum of sound, he protected his face and carefully stood at the entrance of the cave to see what was happening. Then out of the silence God addressed him again, "What are you doing *here*, Elijah?" . . . [15-17]And the Lord told him that it was not on the mountain but down in the midst of turmoil that God's work was to be done and where God himself was active. Kings are to be replaced. A prophet must be commissioned. Judgment will come. [18]But in spite of Elijah's claim that he alone is left in the land as Yahweh's faithful servant, God says he will spare from his judgment that multitude which has remained true to him.

7. THEOLOGIES OF THE PASSAGE

Several of the theologies summarized above, especially that which seems to be the original purpose of the passage and that of the Deuteronomistic editors, proclaim that the God of the Bible is not to be found in or as natural phenomena or in sacred places. Rather he is present for men in his Word which is active in history. Nothing can make that proclamation clearer than the message that this Word became flesh to dwell among us. The presence of God in his Incarnate Word makes sacred places, sacred objects, and theophanic signs idolatrous. This is not to say that church buildings are useless or unimportant, but it is to say that God is present to confront men in such structures and anywhere else when his Word is proclaimed and his will carried out. While several other sermons are possible on the basis of other interpretations of the passage, this concern about the presence of God and his work among men seems most important from the standpoint of the text and from a variety of situations which a Christian preacher must address.

Genesis

28:10–17 (22)

1. ESTABLISHING A WORKING TEXT

There are three major problems which appear when comparing the translations of *RSV*, *NEB*, and *The Torah*, and a literal translation from the Hebrew of this passage raises precisely the same issues. Therefore, such a literal rendering of the whole text is not presented here, but, where helpful, my own translation of particular problems will be included in the comparison.

Any one of the three translations used in this comparison might be used as a working text. However, the substantive differences which should be borne in mind are as follows:

> Verse 12: *RSV*: "... there was a ladder set up on the earth. ..."
> *NEB*: "he saw a ladder, which rested on the ground."
> *Torah*: "... a stairway was set on the ground. ..."

The Torah adds in a footnote that an alternate translation is "ramp." That alternative most clearly approximates the Hebrew where *sullām* seems to mean a "mound."

> Verse 13: *RSV*: "... the Lord stood above it. ..."
> *NEB*: "The Lord was standing beside him. ..."
> *Torah*: "And the Lord was standing beside him. ..."

RSV, in a footnote, allows the possibility of reading "beside him," and likewise in a note, *NEB* recognizes as possible "on it" or "by it." The difficulty here is due to the ambiguity of the Hebrew preposition *'al* which can be translated according to all these possibilities and even more. Such a variation in a preposition, while at first glance insignificant, is crucial to observe and then examine, because the question of God's standing *above* or *on* the mound or *beside* Jacob betrays a certain view of God: transcendent or immanent. Such a distinction, among other things, is related to the analysis of sources.

> Verse 14: *RSV*: ". . . shall all families of the earth bless themselves."
>
> *NEB*: ". . . shall pray to be blessed as you and your descendants are blessed."
>
> *Torah*: "All the families of the earth shall bless themselves. . . ."

The problem here, further complicated by including *AV*'s "be blessed," has again to do with the ambiguity of the Hebrew verb form which can be translated as a passive or as a reflexive.

2. LITERARY MATTERS

Verse 12: "stairway," "ladder," or "ramp." Unfortunately, the form of the Hebrew word which appears here occurs nowhere else in the Old Testament. It does seem, though, that *sullām* comes from a verb meaning "lift up, cast up." That verb is used for casting up a highway (Isa. 62:10), siege works (Job 19:12), and heaps (Jer. 50:26). A related noun, derived from the same verb, *sōlᵉlāh* means a mound used in besieging a city (2 Kings 19:32 which is identical to Isa. 37:33; Jer. 6:6; Ezek. 4:2; 26:8). Thus, on the basis of the meaning of the verb and of the uses of the related noun, *sullām* seems to mean a "heap" or "mound" rather than a ladder.

The translation of the term *sullām* as "mound" brings to mind a pyramidal tower which was popular as a temple tower among the Babylonians and known as a *ziggurat*. These temple towers (cf. Gen. 11:1–9) were constructed in order to reach up to heaven, and in this way they served as the places of communication between the heavenly and earthly worlds. By climbing up to the highest levels of these towers, men could approach the gods for worship and with petitions. Among the Canaanites, such places of intercourse between gods and men were not such ornate towers but nevertheless impressive mounds known as "high places" which served as sanctuaries and upon which altars and cultic symbols were constructed.

Old Testament scholars almost universally agree that Jacob's vision of a "mound" is related to such cultic places. However, while recognizing this mound which reaches up to heaven as a Near Eastern worship site, the interpreter must at the same time recognize that in the Old Testament man does not "climb Jacob's ladder." At Gen. 11:1-9, the story of the Tower of Babel, God stops the construction and disperses the people so that they will not climb up to him; rather the emphasis in that story is that God comes down to men. Likewise in our story, it is not men but God's messengers (angels) who go up and down on the mound. In this way the Old Testament has reinterpreted the old mound concept in such a way as to announce that the biblical God is one who comes to men and not one whom men approach.

Verse 13: "above it" or "beside him." As indicated above, the translation of the preposition betrays a certain view of God: if he stands *above* the mound or *on it*, then he is aloof from Jacob (transcendent); if he stands *beside* Jacob, then, of course, he is immanent. Since the Hebrew preposition *'al* is itself ambiguous, the exegete must seek to determine by a word study of the combination "stand beside/upon" which of the alternatives is most probable. Even this method, however, leads to ambiguous results. While *nissab 'al* usually refers to men standing *beside* things (Gen. 24:13, 43; Exod. 7:15; 18:14; Num. 23:6, 17; Prov. 8:2; Isaiah 21:8) or *beside* persons (Gen. 45:1; 1 Sam. 4:20; 22:6, 7, 9, 17), the expression also seems to be used for persons standing *upon* things (Exod. 33:21?; 34:2; 17:9). In only two of the cases where the combination occurs is Yahweh the subject: Amos 7:7 portrays Yahweh standing *beside* a wall, and Amos 9:1, *beside* an altar. Now herein lies the ambiguity of the results of our word study: whenever the combination *nissab 'al* is used with Yahweh as the subject (as in Gen. 28:13), the preposition means "beside" rather than "upon." However, in those two cases in Amos, Yahweh is standing beside objects rather than men. Nowhere in the Old Testament is Yahweh portrayed as standing beside a man; but nowhere either is he described as standing above an object.

Therefore, the decision must be based on grounds other than

comparable word usage, and to do so we must say a word about source analysis. We have seen in our examination of Genesis 22 that one of the major characteristics of the E source, apart from its use of the name Elohim, is its understanding of the transcendence of God. Contrariwise, our study of Gen. 32:22–32 included a description of the J source which designates the deity by the name Yahweh and often portrays him in rather anthropomorphic terms. For J, Yahweh is an immanent deity who is forever getting himself involved in the affairs of men. If we could decide on the source of verse 13, then the translation of the preposition would take care of itself: E would never describe God as standing beside a man; J would probably not describe him as standing above a mound. Since the subject of our questionable expression is Yahweh and not Elohim, and since his speech of introduction uses Yahweh ("I am the Lord"), the verse seems to be J. Thus the prepositional phrase should be translated "beside him" rather than "above it." Such a portrayal of Yahweh, without the same terminology, is used by J to describe his presence with men at Gen. 18:1 ff. and 32:22–32.

Verse 14: The blessing formula has been discussed above in connection with Gen. 22:18. See the examination of that passage for details.

Verse 17: "house of God" and "gate of heaven." Jacob's vision enabled him to awake from his sleep with the realization that he was in a holy place. His exclamation that this place was "a house of God" (the translation "the house of God" is debatable) certainly is leading up to the naming of that place as Bethel ("house of God") in verse 19. Jacob's further description of the place as "the gate of heaven" is quite understandable in light of what was said above concerning the mound. Since the mound (a *ziggurat*, a high place) is the point of contact between the heavenly and earthly worlds, then that site can appropriately be named "the gate of heaven."

To stop the passage at this point, as the lectionaries do, is to put undue emphasis on Jacob's exclamation of surprise. The passage, as it is listed, however, includes both a theophany and a set of promises—enough indeed to construct a sermon or two. But it is clear that the report of the incident goes on to include some activity and a speech by Jacob in verses 18–22, and so the scope of the passage exceeds verse 17. In the additional five verses, Jacob sets up and anoints a pillar (a Canaanite symbol) in order to designate the spot as a holy place, changes the name of the place to Bethel, and then proceeds to make a vow that if God bring him back safely to his father's house, he will worship Yahweh and tithe all of his possessions.

3. SETTING IN LIFE

Because of the nature of this passage, the settings in life will be discussed under source and redaction criticism. It is sufficient to repeat here that the common ancient Near Eastern cultic concept of a sanctuary as a place of contact with the divine world is attested (but reinterpreted) in this text.

4. THE CRITICISMS

Source analysis of the passage reveals some interesting data for interpretation. Almost all scholars assign verses 11–12, 17–22 to E, and verses 13–16 to J. Verse 10 is variously assigned to J, E, or to a later editor who used it as a transition piece from the previous passage to the present one. Such an assignment of sources, however, seems to me to be oversimplified, and as a result, the importance of the passage in terms of tradition history is diminished.

The Elohistic source indeed comprises verses 11–12 and 17–19a. To read these verses together provides a complete story which bears the marks of E throughout. The name for the deity in verse 12 is Elohim (God); since he is transcendent, God uses mediators to relate to men; frequently God comes to men in visions and dreams. All these characteristics distinguish verse 12 as E, and since verse 11 has no meaning apart from the following verse, it too must be E. Verse 17 continues the marks of E: man's fear before God, the awesomeness of a vision, and again the use of the name Elohim. Verse 18 picks up the action and elements of verse 12 and must likewise be E. The first half of verse 19 provides what seems to be the climax of E's narrative by recording the origin of the name Bethel, one of the favorite sanctuaries of the northern storyteller.

J's story probably includes verses 10, 13–14, and perhaps a portion of verse 16. The record of the journey from Beer-sheba toward Haran (verse 10) is directly related to the preceding narrative of J at 27:41–45 (27:46–28:9 is clearly P). After Jacob had thoroughly aroused the anger of his brother, their mother Rebekah sent the cheater off to Haran to stay with her brother Laban. Our story begins with that journey and is thus J. As for verse 13, the Yahwist is identifiable here, first, by the twofold use of the name Yahweh (the Lord); the Elohist does not use the name Yahweh in a self-introduction or in a narrative until that name is revealed to Moses at Exod. 3:14. Second, the promise of land to the patriarchs is of particular interest to J; E is concerned, it seems, only about the promise of descendants.

Verse 14 continues the promise to include descendants, but because that promise is then tied up with the blessing formula, the verse must be J. Verse 16 seems to belong to the Yahwist, at least in part, because of the name Yahweh in Jacob's exclamation and because it forms a needless repetition with verse 17. (Such repetitions or parallels are one of the signs of conflation of sources.) The problem with the assignment of the whole verse to J is that the reference to Jacob's waking from sleep occurs without reference to his going to sleep (verse 11 was E.) Moreover, it is not one of the marks of J to describe Yahweh as coming to men in dreams. It seems then that "Then Jacob awoke from his sleep" belongs with verse 17 which records his fear (E) and that Jacob's speech in verse 16 (probably J) is simply his verbal response to the promise he had just heard. The redactor who combined J and E moved some of the material around in order to make one story out of two separate ones.

Thus far we have not assigned verses 15, 19a–22 to any source. None of the characteristics of J or E is present here. On the contrary, all the key phrases and expressions seem to be D (the Deuteronomistic school of the exilic period). Verse 15 contains God's promise that he will be with Jacob: "I am with you" occurs more than twenty times in the Old Testament, more than half of which appear in the Deuteronomistic history. More important than that expression by itself, however, is the combination of that promise with "in all the way that you go" (cf. Josh. 1:9) and with "I will not forsake you" (Deut. 31:6, 8; Josh. 1:5). That these combinations occur only in the Deuteronomistic corpus and in verse 15 of our text seems to indicate that the author of Gen. 28:15 is D. Furthermore, while no exact equivalent to "until I have accomplished that which I promised you," the content sounds very much like the Deuteronomistic concept of the Word of the Lord as effecting the fulfillment of his promises.[1] Finally, the promise "I will bring you back" is a favorite expression of the Deuteronomists in the prose sections of the Book of Jeremiah where it is addressed to the exiles in Babylon (see Jer. 12:15; 16:15; 23:3; 24:6; 27:22; 9:14; 30:3; 32:37; 33:7).[2]

While the first half of verse 19 has already been assigned to E, the parenthetical expression "but the name of the city was . . . at the first" is paralleled only in the Deuteronomistic passage at Judg. 18:29. From this point on, the rest of the passage—Jacob's vow— is D. To begin with, the Hebrew reads literally, "Then Jacob vowed a vow." This seemingly redundant expression appears in exactly the same form in a number of passages which belong to the Deuteronomists (Deut. 12:17; 23:22, 23, 24; Judg. 11:30, 39; 1 Sam. 1:11; 2 Sam. 15:7, 8; Jer. 44:25). Other passages where the same expression occurs are unidentifiable as regards source or are generally recognized as late (Num. 6:2, 21; 21:2; 30:3, 4; Isa. 19:21). Even more interesting are some of the elements in several of D's "vow a vow" sayings. The expression at 1 Sam. 1:11 introduces a deal which Hannah makes with the Lord, as Jacob does in our text. At Judg. 11:30, 39 appears Jephthah's bargain with the Lord, also introduced by "vow a vow."

Most interesting, however, is 2 Sam. 15:7–8: ". . . Absalom said to the king, 'Let me go and pay my vow which I have vowed to the Lord in Hebron. For while I lived at Geshur in Aram, your servant vowed a vow, "If the Lord will indeed bring me back to Jerusalem, then I will offer worship to the Lord in this place." This last example is strikingly similar to Jacob's vow at Gen. 28:20–22: (1) the expression "vow a vow"; (2) the condition of returning at the will and action of the Lord; (3) the promise to

---

1. See Gerhard von Rad, *Studies in Deuteronomy*, "Studies in Biblical Theology," no. 9, trans. David Stalker (London: SCM Press, 1953), pp. 74–91.

2. For the arguments that the Deuteronomists are responsible for the prose section of Deuteronomy, see E. W. Nicholson, *Preaching to the Exiles* (New York: Schocken Books, 1970).

worship Yahweh upon return. Finally, but also significant among the "vow a vow" sayings, is Deut. 12:17 where the vow is combined with the regulation concerning the tithe. Nowhere else in the Old Testament does this combination occur except for Jacob's vow in our passage.

Furthermore, within this vow the expression "Yahweh will be to me as God" is a favorite expression of D (Deut. 26:17; 29:12; Judg. 8:33; 2 Sam. 7:24; Jer. 7:23; 11:4; 30:22; 24:7; 31:33; 32:38). Apart from D the expression occurs almost exclusively in exilic or post-exilic texts (mostly P and Ezekiel, neither of which have anything to do with our passage.)

5. CONTEXT

The preceding source analysis now leads us to deal with form, redaction, and tradition criticism—each of which disciplines has something of significance for the interpretation of our passage.

The Elohist's version of the story is a theophany narrative or cult legend which is used as an etiology: it explains the origin and the name of the sanctuary at Bethel. Since most scholars agree that Bethel was probably a Canaanite sanctuary before it was used for the worship of Yahweh, it is not unlikely that this cultic etiology existed among the Canaanites with one of their heroes of antiquity as the recipient of the "mound" vision. The significance of the mound can best be understood from this environment anyway. If the story was indeed connected to the cultic site of the Canaanites originally, then the Elohist redacted that story in such a way that the hero became Jacob and that God's angels traveled up and down the ramp. Thus, the old cult site would have been legitimized for the worship of Yahweh by the Israelites. Since Bethel was one of the two sites selected by Jeroboam when the northern kingdom separated itself from Judah (see 1 Kings 12), such a story as this would have authenticated the site as *kosher* for Israelite worship. In the midst of this concern for a particular cultic site, however, the Elohist tells us something about God: *Precisely because God is transcendent and cannot be reached, he comes to men to establish relationship and to call men to worship.*

The Yahwistic version of the story seems to have nothing to do with Bethel. Nor does the Yahwist record a theophany of any sort.

Rather his narrative is a saga in which God intervened in the life of Jacob as he fled from Beer-sheba to Haran. It was J who had just recorded the reason for Jacob's flight as due to the patriarch's cheating of his brother (Gen. 27:41–45). Now, as was so typical of J, he records that to Jacob, the cunning refugee, God continued to reiterate the promise he had made to Abraham and to Isaac years before. Thus J's proclamation about God is: *Even to the most rebellious of men, God announces his faithfulness to the promise he has made.*

The JE redactor put the two proclamations together in such a way that the promise to Jacob occurred within the context of the theophany at Bethel. The combined account seems to proclaim: *When the transcendent God appears to his people, he communicates by speaking his Word of promise even to the most unlikely of men.*

For the Deuteronomist the passage had other possibilities. As we noted in the discussion on 1 Kings 19:9–18, D had to address the exiles in Babylon with a God who was not tied down to unreachable holy places or to destroyed holy architecture. He had to proclaim that God was present apart from the territory of Judah and Israel, that he came to his people wherever they were in his Word. The situation of Jacob in Gen. 28:10 ff. suited his needs perfectly. Jacob, like the nation later, was exiled from his homeland because of his wicked deeds; furthermore, he was on his way to Mesopotamia (Haran) where he, like the exiles later, would sojourn for some time. But the Lord appeared to him as he was leaving his homeland and promised to give him the land where he lay. To this promise of land—which itself was important for D—the Deuteronomist added the promise of verse 15 which declared that Yahweh would go with him wherever he went, that he would not forsake him, that he would bring him back to accomplish his promise. Jacob, in other words, was Israel in exile, to whom God promises his presence in a foreign land and the return of the people to their own land.

Furthermore, continuing to add to the story, D supplemented the vow at verses 20–22 in order to demonstrate to the exiles that when God makes this promise to the forefather Jacob, the patriarch promises that, upon return to the land, Yahweh and none other will be his God, and that he will worship and thank him by giving him a tenth of all that he has. This vow is not really an offensive deal by Jacob at all! God has already promised that he will care for the patriarch and bring him home (verse 15). Thus Jacob's vow really means: "Since God will be with me . . ., my repsonse will be one of worship and praise and tithe." According to D's understanding of the effectiveness of the spoken Word of God, once the promise is made by the Lord in verse 15, there can be no "if's." This vow serves to show the exiles that, like Jacob, they should respond to God's promise by exclusive worship of Yahweh and by tithing to him all that they have.

Thus the Deuteronomists took the old tradition about "Jacob's ladder" and reinterpreted it in such a way that it spoke not of a sacred place but of God's presence in a foreign land and of his promise of the exiles' return to receive the land as their own. Further, as recipients of this gracious word, they are to worship him and him alone as God. Thus D's proclamation to the exiles was: *The transcendent God whom our forefathers worshiped at certain places is present for his people in his word wherever they are, to protect them and lead them home, in response to which they will worship him as God.*

6. INTERPRETATIVE RENDERING

On the basis of the preceding investigation, the old familiar "ladder" of verse 12 should be rendered as "mound." The prepositional problem in verse 13 should read "the Lord stood beside him," and the blessing formula (on the basis of our study of Gen. 22:18) can be paraphrased "and because of your descendants shall all the nations of the earth consider themselves fortunate." Beyond these literary problems noted in the work of establishing the text, we have seen that the "if" of Jacob's vow at verse 20 should be changed to "since" on the basis of D's understanding of the effectiveness of the Word of God. Apart from these few comments, the working text can stand as it is for the interpretative rendering.

7. THEOLOGIES OF THE PASSAGE

The text, as interpreted above, obviously meant many things to many people as it was passed on in the traditions of Israel. The

Elohist's cult legend or etiology, as redacted by that writer, proclaims that *the God of the Bible, unlike the gods of religion, reaches out to men to establish a relationship with them*. Such a proclamation is, of course, quite consistent with the New Testament witness to the Word of God which became man in order to unite us with himself. The one problem I have with E's theology at this point is that God *appears* for the Elohist rather than speaks; E does not emphasize the Word, as do J, D, and the New Testament witnesses.

The Yahwist's proclamation that *God announces his faithfulness to the promises he has made, even to the most rebellious of his people* is quite meaningful for Christian proclamation. The New Testament makes abundantly clear that God sent his Son to die for sinners, that he accepts us not because of what we do but in spite of ourselves. Furthermore, this act of God comes about by the proclamation of his Word which is effective in our lives.

The testimony of the JE redactor combines *the transcendence of God with his communication to unworthy men by his Word of promise*. This combination relieves the problem with E's method of describing the coming of God in visions and, at the same time, preserves E's concern for transcendence and J's understanding of God's faithful promise even to sinners.

Finally, the use of the tradition by the Deuteronomists provides a powerful message for the church today. The apparent absence of God in our times has given rise to the recent "God is dead" movement on the one hand and to the popular futurist theologians on the other. The Deuteronomist proclaims to an apparently God-forsaken situation, not that God died a long time ago or that he is in the process of becoming, but that *God is indeed present with his people in his Word wherever they are, to protect them and lead them home, in response to which they worship him as God*. In Word Incarnate God is present whenever sermons are preached, sacraments administered, or Christians console one another with the good news. Our Father brings home his prodigal sons and summons us to praise him in word and deed for his faithfulness to his promise which he has fulfilled in his only Son.

APPENDIX

SERMONS FROM

OLD TESTAMENT TEXTS

Genesis

32:22–32

(The following sermon was addressed to the community of a Lutheran theological seminary. The text was selected because this pericope was then designated for the First Sunday after Easter, during which week the sermon was delivered in the chapel. Because the academic year would end in a few weeks and each member of the student community would then launch out into a new, exciting, and yet fearsome venture, I selected as the most appropriate level of proclamation that of the JE redactor which placed emphasis on the context of the story. This context speaks of Jacob's encounter with God the night before the patriarch met his brother Esau from whom he fled many years earlier.)

One of the greatest disservices we can do to ourselves is to think we can become "buddies" with God. As strange as it seems, the result of an overfamiliarity with God is that it really makes little difference in our lives whether he is with us or not as we face challenges, heartbreaks, and those ever-demanding crises that are upon us. If God is just another friend, even the friendliest of friends, then frankly you and I would do better to confide in the flesh and blood buddies around us than to worry about this spiritual friend who is always so elusive and ambiguous anyway. But, if he's something more than a buddy, look out!

More often than we like, crises do come along to complicate our lives. The moment of vocational decision is upon some of you as you look to the imminent end of the academic year. For some of you, this means a decision concerning the ordained ministry; for others the diaconate; for others, still something else. Or the crisis may be a family or personal disharmony in which it has become difficult to face another person because of something you've said or done. And for all of you, there is a new situation in life just around the corner: a twelve-week program of Clinical Pastoral Education where you will see suffering you might never have seen before; an internship in a parish which is unknown to you and under a supervisor you've met only superficially; or the responsibility of being an officially ordained pastor of the church where you can no longer plead that you're only a student.

In any case there are several ways in which you and I *can* face such crises. We might choose the way of positive thinking, convincing ourselves that we are certainly up to the challenge, that such a situation is no match for the like of you and me. Or again, we might opt for ignoring the problem, pretending it simply isn't there, so that eventually it will take care of itself. Or perhaps a clever scheme of some sort will take the heat off us and the burden of decision or action will conveniently fall on someone else.

Yet, there's still another way to face such a crisis, the only legitimate way as far as the Bible is concerned. Our lesson from Genesis 32 puts it something like this: In the midst of the crises of life, God comes to wrestle with us to change us, so that we might face the problem as different persons. And what a strange story it is that tells this message! Jacob had just pulled off one more feat of deception. He managed to run off from his father-in-law Laban, taking with him most of what had been near and dear to his in-laws: their daughters, their grandchildren, a good portion of their flocks, and the rights to the primary share of the inheritance. Jacob had masterminded the whole scheme. He made a deal with his father-in-law that he would be kind enough to take the blemished animals from Laban's flock, so that the herd would remain pure. Then by magical trickery Jacob managed to blemish most of the herd. Now when Laban was off in the field one day with his sons, Jacob left with all that he could muster in his caravan. Ultimately, the enraged Laban caught up with the fugitives, but Jacob talked his way out of the situation, bade farewell to his father-in-law, and continued on his way.

But this way was the real crisis for Jacob, because he was headed toward his brother Esau. Esau too had been the victim of his brother's schemes. Years before, Jacob robbed his twin of his birthright and of his blessing. He was gone for almost fourteen years, and now he was returning to confront his brother. The old cheater was about to face the greatest crisis of his life. He sent his family ahead with all the flocks, and Jacob remained alone on the other side of the river. And there, before the crisis, in Jacob's solitude, God came to wrestle with him. And wrestle they did—all through the night until day was about to break. Then strangely, when the match was nearly over, the visitor asked Jacob his name. And when he was told what it was, the wrestler changed Jacob's name to Israel. Then Jacob asked the visitor his name, but in a flash the opponent was gone, leaving Jacob a blessing but no name. It was then that it occurred to our hero that the "man" he had wrestled all night long was none other than God himself.

At first glance the story sounds like an ancient Semitic version of Billy Goats Gruff. Just as the little goats had to battle the ogre before crossing the bridge, so Jacob had to fight a demon of some sort before he could cross the river. But, in fact, the story has a profound message about God and his effect on men. For Old Testament man, the *name* of a person was much more than a handle to identify someone; the name, in fact, *was* the person. If one man knew another's name, he had some power and control over him— precisely because the name and the person were identical. Or, if a person's name were changed, then the person himself was changed, too, because the two—name and person—were the same. Now in this story God comes in the form of a man to wrestle with Jacob and to change his name. According to brother Esau, "Jacob" meant "he cheats," for Esau said one time, "You are rightly named Jacob, for you have cheated me twice." But now God makes Jacob different by changing his name to Israel. Now Jacob moves on to face his crisis as a man who has been changed by an encounter with God.

What difference did it make the next day when Jacob crossed the river and stood face to face with his brother? All the difference in the world! Jacob approached his brother with gifts, bowing down seven times in humility and offering to his brother everything that he had. All this from Jacob, "the cheater"? Impossible!

These words are from Israel, the Jacob who has been confronted by God.

It just might make a difference in your life and in mine that God comes to confront us, to wrestle with us in our doubts and fears, in our ever present crises. It might make a difference because by such an encounter God will make *us* different to face the problem. That's partly what Easter is all about. The resurrection of Jesus Christ is the means by which God comes to confront us; he comes in his living and glorious Son who is our Lord. But be careful! He comes often to wrestle us down and change us; he comes whenever other people bear him witness. Whenever someone carries the message that God sent his Son to die on our behalf, he comes to encounter us. In sermons, yes! In the liturgy, yes! In the sacraments, yes! But most often, and most frightening, in the daily conversations of Christians with one another. That is what is known as the good news.

Now for the bad news. When he comes and when the struggle has taken place, then there is no possibility of facing the crisis by positive thinking or by ignoring the problem in hopes that it will solve itself. Jacob had none of those options. And neither do we once we are confronted by God who is not our buddy but our Lord. He sends us smack into the heart of the matter, but he sends us as different persons. No buddy can do that. Equipped by his presence and his blessing to face what needs to be done, we move ahead into those frightening situations.

Now there are three important things to remember about this God who confronts us. First, if the situation is no longer as frightening as it had been before, surely it is not because we have God in our hip pockets whom we can pull out for escape when the going gets rough. When the first woman screams in that mental institution in which you are working this summer, God will not transplant you back here to a comfortable pew. God is not at your control or mine to do with as we please. This strange story about God and Jacob makes crystal clear that while God gains control over Jacob by learning his name and then changing him, Jacob is never told the name of his adversary. He never gets control over God. All that he received was an obscure blessing—apparently that God had made him different and had placed him under his dominion. But

God maintained his freedom and his power. He always remains in control when he encounters us. That's first.

And this is second. The God whom we know as the father of Jesus Christ will come to us in the face of crises even if we have tried to do without him in the past, if we have pretended, like Jacob, that we could handle the problems of life on our own. He comes to encounter us even if we have made a mess of things before, or if we have done nothing at all. The professional disasters you might have experienced as interns when you tried to do it on your own will not keep him away when similar trials appear again. God comes to you to wrestle with you, so that this time you might be different.

There's still a third thing to remember about the God who confronts us in his Word. The result of his wrestling, of his changing us, is not that we become automatic winners in the games of life. After our bout with God, there's no invincibility about you and me; there's no impossibility of failing to be successful. Jacob did not win out over Esau. He met his brother humbly, like a servant before a master, ready to give rather than receive. What God does give in his wrestling is his judging and cleansing presence which transforms us again and again according to his will. That transformation might indeed make a difference in the way you handle that personal or family feud.

And so it is, in the face of the problems which so frequently confront you, God comes, not as a smiling buddy who OK's whatever you plan. Rather he comes in the resurrected Christ, whenever he is proclaimed, to play the game of Billy Goats Gruff. He blocks you on the way to the problem—but only for a while. Only long enough to wrestle a bit, so that this time he might make you different. And when the struggle is through, he will remain in complete control. But in his own peculiar way, God will give you his own peculiar kind of victory to face the crises of your lives.

Genesis

22:1–19

(On the First Sunday in Lent I preached this sermon to a suburban congregation with which I am quite familiar. As I studied the various theologies of the text, I decided to use as the basis for the sermon the proclamation of the whole passage as it stands in its present context. The reasons for this decision were twofold: (1) Lent, which looks toward the crucifixion, presents an apparent contradiction for the Messiah was not supposed to die; (2) the emphasis in the passage on the demand for Abraham to be different from his neighbors spoke to the problem of religiosity which is so prominent in suburban society.)

We stand at the beginning of another Lenten season when we are to prepare our hearts and minds for the suffering and death of Jesus. Preparation is indeed necessary, for what we are up against in his suffering is nothing less than "the great contradiction of the Bible." When the Old Testament speaks of a Messiah who would come to rule over God's kingdom, there is never any hint that this Messiah or Christ would suffer—to say nothing of die. And yet Jesus, the Messiah, the Christ, looms before us these days all but naked, bleeding and exhausted, hanging on a cross. The Messiah who was not supposed to suffer dies this humiliating death set for criminals. This is the Bible's great contradiction.

The experiences of our lives, in fact, present us with a number of cases in which God seems to be contradicting himself. We are led to believe that when God would send his Messiah, things worldly would be rosy and sublime. The promise of a peaceful kingdom where the wolf and lamb dwell together, where swords are beaten into plowshares, where wickedness is obliterated and all men are treated justly—this promise seems to be a farfetched dream as we look at the world around us. In the Middle East, while the sounds of guns and bombs are silent at the moment, the tension there and the possibility of real fireworks are ever present. In Indochina, while our troops are finally being withdrawn, the situation is far from peaceful. In Ireland the people of the church—Christians—fight against each other like some mad scene from the Middle Ages. In our own land, in spite of our Constitution and Bill of Rights, justice is not for everyone, it seems, for a black man when arrested is treated differently from a white man in the same situation; or a multimillionaire pays no income taxes; or the victim of a crime bears his own loss while the culprit is set free on a legality. All this goes on in spite of the fact that the New Testament tells us that the kingdom of God is here, that the Messiah has come to rule over it. God seems to be caught in a whole bundle of contradictions.

Our Old Testament lesson for this First Sunday in Lent is one of the most refined, and at the same time most moving, stories in the Bible. It is a story which has meant many things to many people. At first it may have been told to show the people of Israel that they should not sacrifice their children—as the Canaanites did. To someone else the story told about God's testing faith. Yet the story has still another meaning when we see it in light of the whole story about Abraham.

When God first appeared to Abraham somewhere in Mesopotamia, he told the patriarch to go to a foreign land where God would make him a great nation and would cause him to be a blessing for all families of the earth. In that foreign land, Abraham managed to get himself into all kinds of trouble. He became involved in a war with several powerful kings; twice, in order to save his own life, he told foreign kings that his beautiful wife Sarah was only his sister (he was afraid of what they'd do to rid her of her husband); at one point he even had a debate with God about what the Lord intended to do to Sodom and Gomorrah. But through it all, through Abraham's belligerence, his arrogance, and his outright deceit, God kept promising him that he would become

a great nation. The Lord kept up the promise that Abraham and
Sarah would have a son.

Now Abraham, we are told, was seventy-five years old when
God first appeared to him in Mesopotamia; eighty-six years old
when Sarah gave to her husband the servant girl Hagar, so that
Abraham could have a son through her. And now Abraham was
one hundred years old and still waiting for his ninety-nine-year-old
wife to bear him their own son. It's no wonder that when God
came again to repeat the promise of that son that the old couple
laughed in his face! They had absolutely no biological right to
have a child; at this stage they could claim nothing about themselves which would enable them to have a son. But that was the
point. When they were firmly convinced that they could not have a
child, *then* God gave them their son—a pure gift, a gift due only
to the promise and faithfulness of God.

Now watch what happens. The birth of Isaac is recorded in the
twenty-first chapter of Genesis. One chapter later God appears to
Abraham and says, "Take your son, your only son, Isaac, whom
you love, and go to the land of Moriah, and offer him there as a
burnt offering upon one of the mountains of which I shall tell
you." Imagine it! Abraham waited until he was more than a
hundred years old to have his son, and before we are told of the
joyous experiences a father and son can have together, God asked
Abraham to give him back.

In a sense it was not too startling a demand. Abraham's neighbors, the Canaanites regularly sacrificed their children, and so God
was asking Abraham to do what his neighbors did. Of course, it
made no sense to Abraham, for how could God fulfill his promise
if he now took away the first of the many descendants to come? To
Abraham it could only seem that God was contradicting himself;
he was taking away the blessing he had promised for so long. Nevertheless, Abraham did what God had commanded.

When father and son arrived at the appointed spot, Abraham
placed Isaac on the altar he had made. Then just as Abraham was
about to bring down the knife, God called him to stop, com-
mended Abraham for his faith, and provided a ram for the sacrifice. As a finale, God reiterated his promise that through his descendants Abraham would become a great nation and all nations

would somehow experience blessing. What happened in the story is this: through his apparent contradiction God brought Abraham to commit himself in faith, strengthening and refining the relationship between them and enabling Abraham to know who he was in his world.

God, you see, didn't contradict himself at all. He simply used his apparent contradiction to pull Abraham closer to himself and thus to establish for Abraham his identity as one faithful to a different kind of God and separate from the world in which he lived. In that sense the story speaks to us in several ways.

In the first place, God uses the apparent contradictions of life to call you and me to faith. That's not to say that he causes the tragedies and problems of our lives simply to see how we will react. That wasn't the case with Abraham: no tragedy occurred. And it's not the case with us. The tragedies that you and I and all the rest of men experience are due to the presence and power of sin in the world—that rebellion of every man against the God who made us which has affected the way we act toward him, toward one another, the way our world turns in chaos, the pollution of our health, our air, our streams, and all other tragedies which occur. But because we constantly mix up God with an impersonal divine providence which is the cause of everything that happens, God gets the blame for all the tragedies and is thus accused of contradicting the promise of peace in his kingdom. Yet, in the midst of the tragedies and tensions of our lives which are the result of man's rebellion, God calls you and me to trust in him, to confide in his promise that in spite of all appearances to the contrary, his peace and comfort are available to those who believe.

Second, your belief in the promise of God in spite of apparent contradictions makes you distinct from the world. For Abraham this distinction consisted of confidence in a God who did not demand the sacrifice of children, as did the gods of the Canaanites, a God, in fact, who continued his promise precisely by preventing the sacrifice of Isaac. For you this distinction from the world consists of confidence in a God who became man, who suffered and died because of the power of sin in the world, who so loved the world that he gave *his* only son for the likes of us.

Third, being distinct from the world does not mean to leave it, but rather to be one of God's instruments of blessing in and to the world. Just before our story about Abraham and Isaac began, we are told that Abraham lived in Beer-sheba. And at the end of our story we read, "So Abraham returned to his young men, and they arose and went together to Beer-sheba; and Abraham dwelt at Beer-sheba." Abraham's distinctness from the world around him did not mean that he was escorted to the clouds. Rather he went home, lived among the Canaanites, so that God could fulfill his promise that, through his descendants, all nations of the earth would experience God's blessing. Called to be different, called to be the church, you and I cannot leave the world or ignore it. On the contrary, God sends us into the world, into the apparent contradictions, so that he can use us to reach others, to call others to faith as he calls us.

The history of the church shows a movement between two extremes. There have been times when the church has been different in the sense that it was a refuge, a retreat from the world, a kind of otherworldly center where Christians could escape the harsh realities of life. But there have also been times when the church recognized no difference at all between itself and the world, and simply understood itself as one more institution among many. To a certain extent, both these extremes exist today—an unhealthy exclusivism from the world on the one hand and an unholy identification with the world on the other.

God calls you to faith in himself and in his promise. That faith makes you distinct, to be sure. But at the same time, he sends you into the world with a mission to be his instrument of blessing. What makes you different and what you take to the world is a message, and the message is this: the Great Contradiction of the Bible, that the Christ suffers and dies, is God's means of drawing all men to himself. Indeed, when it came to his Son, his only Son, God did not spare the knife, or the nails, or the whip, or the spear. But he remained faithful nevertheless, for in his Son he established his kingdom, and he raised that Son to be the living Lord of our lives. It is to that faith that he calls you, and it is with that message that he sends you out into the contradictions of life.